D0769253

Theodore Dreiser Revisited

Twayne's United States Authors Series

Joseph M. Flora, Editor
University of North Carolina

TUSAS 614

Theodore Dreiser. Courtesy The Theodore Dreiser Collection, Special Collections, Van Pelt Library, University of Pennsylvania.

Theodore Dreiser Revisited

Philip Gerber

The State University of New York

Twayne Publishers ■ New York

Maxwell Macmillan Canada ■ Toronto

Maxwell Macmillan International ■ New York Oxford Singapore Sydney

Theodore Dreiser Revisited
Philip Gerber

Twayne Publishers   Maxwell Macmillan Canada, Inc.
Macmillan Publishing Company   1200 Eglinton Avenue East
866 Third Avenue   Suite 200
New York, New York 10022   Don Mills, Ontario M3C 3N1

Macmillan Publishing Company is part of the Maxwell Communications
Group of Companies.

Library of Congress Cataloging-in-Publication Data

Gerber, Philip L.
      Theodore Dreiser revisited / Philip Gerber.
            p. cm. – (Twayne's United States authors series ; TUSAS 523)
      Includes bibliographical references and index.
      ISBN 0-8057-3966-1 (alk. paper) ✓
      1. Dreiser, Theodore, 1871-1945 – Criticism and interpretation.
I. Title. II. Series.
PS3507.R55Z637   1992
813'.52 – dc20   92-7283
                                                            CIP

The paper used in this publication meets the minimum requirements of
American National Standard for Information Sciences – Permanence of
Paper for Printed Library Materials, ANSI Z39.48-1984.

10 9 8 7 6 5 4 3 2 1

Printed in the United States of America.

To Ken Eble, in fond memory

Contents

Preface

When the first edition of this book was composed, a quarter of a century ago, surprisingly little was available on library shelves concerning the life and works of Theodore Dreiser. We had, of course, important pioneering works such as Dorothy Dudley's early critical study *Forgotten Frontiers: Dreiser and the Land of the Free* (1932) and Robert Elias's later ground-breaking biography *Theodore Dreiser: Apostle of Nature* (1949). Both of these works remain among the most valuable studies of Dreiser, in part because their authors had the incalculable advantage of working directly with the novelist himself, in person and over a period of years.

Since 1949 publishers have issued biographical and critical books on Dreiser in a profusion, as part of a post-World War II burgeoning of interest in American writers. This phenomenon is dealt with in my new chapters, which mention many works out of the abundant array now available and central to Dreiser studies. All of these have enhanced the accelerating study of this important American writer's life and contribution to American letters. The concern of these new chapters, in the widest sense, is the persistent and rising swell of critical interest in Theodore Dreiser. Here I lean on the perspective of history as I cite the various types, degrees, and qualities of attention paid the novelist. I also offer an appraisal of secondary works primarily based on my personal judgments (with all my own biases and prejudices), yet concerned as well with reflecting a consensus wherever possible. Omissions and mistakes of wrongheadedness are attributable to me alone, of course, and to my own limitations.

In 1964, establishing a field of vision within which to frame my study of the prolific Dreiser, I quoted Fred Lewis Pattee's remark that "to weigh the man as a force in the period one must begin with his six novels, the rest of his output is but chips and explanations and excursions." As the 1990s begin, I find the truth of that judgment to be essentially undiminished. If it is not precisely accurate to say that Dreiser's other literary works are but "chips" off his novels, it has become evident that the novels, more than ever, form that indispensable center for continued interest in his contribution to American letters. Dreiser's plays, poems, stories, diaries, travel books, and autobiographies, whatever their intrinsic interest as separate works (and in certain instances that interest can be considerable), are most likely to possess enduring value in direct ratio to the degree that they aid in defining the man as citizen and writer, the extent to which they impress a reader with Dreiser's sincerity of philosophical stance and singleness of purpose. It seems incontrovertible now to suggest that Dreiser, given the irrepressible force of his novels alone, can survive rather well as a major American literary figure. Accordingly, Dreiser the novelist continues to be the focus in this revised edition.

Since 1962 I have enjoyed the awesome and indispensable advantage of access to the great Dreiser Collection held at the University of Pennsylvania. Since my first encounter with this collection, Neda M. Westlake, until recently the curator, generously and without stint made available to me Dreiser's manuscripts, correspondence, diaries, unpublished essays and stories, as well as other documents and memorabilia. For this help in fleshing out my understanding of Dreiser in myriad aspects of his life and work, I owe Mrs. Westlake a debt that, like most debts of scholar to scholar, is essentially unpayable. The Dreiser Collection continues to serve; I thank Daniel H. Traister, its present curator, for permission to use the photograph that serves as the frontispiece for this volume. I thank also Liz Fowler, my editor at Twayne Publishers, for her interest and aid; and Joseph M. Flora, the general editor for this series, who has read the manuscript with care and saved me from any number of infelicities.

Since 1971, when I was invited to become a contributing editor to the *Dreiser Newsletter,* it has been my great pleasure to provide the *Newsletter* from time to time with examples of my own research and thinking as well as with my responses to others' newly published works. In its pages I have read with profit the scholarly contributions of many who have caused Dreiser studies to prosper and advance. My association with Richard W. Dowell, the longtime editor of the *Newsletter* (now known as *Dreiser Studies*), has been one of the most significant and pleasant associations of my professional life. In company with Thomas P. Riggio and James L. W. West III, Dick

Dowell read my new chapters and saved me from making any number of errors, and I thank all of them for this assistance.

No work develops in a vacuum, and my own has been aided by Dreiser relatives, friends, biographers, and scholars who in ways often dramatic and sometimes rather subtle have had an impact on my own thinking. Through correspondence or personal contact – and in fortunate instances, both – it has been my great pleasure to be associated with many who share a respect and admiration for Dreiser's achievement. One of those with whom I enjoyed an enduring friendship was Professor Kenneth E. Eble, my one-time colleague at the University of Utah and more recently the Twayne field editor under whose aegis this revision was begun. For many reasons, personal as well as professional, it seems fitting that this volume should be dedicated to his memory.

Chronology

1871   Theodore Dreiser born 27 August in Terre Haute, Indiana.

1879   Family separates; Theodore accompanies mother, Sarah Schanab Dreiser, to Vincennes then to Sullivan, Indiana.

1882   Paul Dreiser arranges housing for the family in Evansville, Indiana.

1883   Family regroups briefly in Chicago.

1883-1887   Family resides in Warsaw, Indiana. Family separates once more.

1887-1889   Dreiser travels alone to Chicago for the first time, works as common laborer in a restaurant and for a hardware company.

1889-1890   Studies at Indiana University, Bloomington.

1890   Death of Dreiser's mother on 14 November.

1892   Dreiser begins newspaper career with position on Chicago *Globe*. In November moves to Saint Louis as reporter for *Globe-Democrat and Republic*.

1893   Meets Sara White during excursion to World's Columbian Exposition in Chicago.

1894   In March, departs Saint Louis for the East; briefly resides in Toledo, Cleveland, and Pittsburgh.

1895   Begins residence in New York in October. Establishment of *Ev'ry Month* (music periodical) with Dreiser as editor. Beginning of Dreiser's magazine career.

1898   Marries Sara White in December.

1899   Spends the summer in Arthur Henry's home, Maumee, Ohio; begins writing fiction, which soon leads to composition of *Sister Carrie* (first novel).

1900	*Sister Carrie* published and suppressed by Doubleday, Page and Company.
1901-1903	Dreiser attempts *Jennie Gerhardt* (novel); suffers an incapacitating emotional collapse.
1904	Becomes fiction editor for Street and Smith publications in July.
1905	Becomes editor of *Smith's Magazine* in April.
1906	Becomes editor of *Broadway Magazine* in April. His favorite brother, Paul Dreiser (Dresser), dies.
1907	*Sister Carrie* republished 18 May by B. W. Dodge and Company.
1909	Dreiser resumes intensive work on *Jennie Gerhardt* (novel). Separates from Sara White Dreiser.
1910	Forced 15 October to sever connections with Butterick publications.
1911	*Jennie Gerhardt* accepted in April by Harper and Brothers. In November, Dreiser travels to Europe to research the career of Charles Tyson Yerkes for *The Financier* (novel).
1912	*The Financier* published by Harper and Brothers as first volume of *A Trilogy of Desire* (novels); *Sister Carrie* republished by Harper and Brothers.
1913	*A Traveler at Forty* (nonfiction) published by the Century Company.
1914	*The Titan,* second volume of *A Trilogy of Desire,* published 15 May by John Lane after rejection by Harpers.
1915	Dreiser revisits boyhood homes in Indiana. In October, *The "Genius"* (novel) published by John Lane.
1916	*Plays of the Natural and the Supernatural* published by John Lane. *The "Genius"* withdrawn in July by John Lane after obscenity charges are filed against it. *A Hoosier Holiday* (autobiography) published by John Lane.

1918	*Free, and Other Stories, The Hand of the Potter* (play), and *Twelve Men* (sketches) published by Boni and Liveright.
1919	Dreiser has first meeting with cousin, Helen Richardson.
1920	*Hey, Rub-a-Dub-Dub!* (philosophy and speculation) published by Boni and Liveright.
1919-1922	Dreiser moves to Hollywood. Beginning of love affair with Helen Richardson. Begins writing *An American Tragedy* (novel).
1922	*A Book about Myself* (autobiography), second volume of projected series *A History of Myself,* published by Boni and Liveright.
1923	*The "Genius"* republished and *The Color of a Great City* (sketches) published by Boni and Liveright. Dreiser moves with Helen to New York to continue work on *An American Tragedy.*
1925	*An American Tragedy* published by Boni and Liveright.
1927	*Chains* (short stories) published by Boni and Liveright. In November, Dreiser travels to Russia; remains as a visitor until January 1928.
1928	*Moods, Cadenced and Declaimed* (poems) and *Dreiser Looks at Russia* published by Boni and Liveright.
1929	*A Gallery of Women* (sketches) published by Horace Liveright.
1930	*Fine Furniture* (long short story) published by Random House.
1931	*Tragic America* (nonfiction) published by Horace Liveright. *Dawn,* first volume of projected *A History of Myself* published by Horace Liveright; *A Book about Myself* republished as *Newspaper Days* by Horace Liveright.
1932-1934	Dreiser acts as coeditor of *American Spectator* magazine; attempts *The Stoic* (novel).

1939   *The Living Thoughts of Thoreau* (edited with introduction by Dreiser) published by Longmans, Green.

1941   *America Is Worth Saving* (nonfiction) published by Horace Liveright.

1942   Sara White Dreiser dies 1 October.

1944   Dreiser accepts Award of Merit from the American Academy of Arts and Letters. Marries Helen Richardson 13 June.

1945   Writes William Z. Foster 20 July applying for membership in Communist party. Dies 28 December in Hollywood, California.

1946   *The Bulwark* (novel) published by Doubleday.

1947   *The Stoic,* third volume of *A Trilogy of Desire,* published by Doubleday. *The Best Short Stories of Theodore Dreiser,* edited by Howard Fast, published by World.

1949   *Theodore Dreiser: Apostle of Nature* by Robert H. Elias – first complete biography, written in consultation with Dreiser – is published by Alfred A. Knopf.

Chapter One

The Well of Memory: Dreiser's Youth

Theodore Dreiser was the first major American author to spring from continental European immigrants.[1] Before Dreiser's time, our literature had been dominated solidly by men of direct Anglo-Saxon lineage, many of them aristocratic by birth, highly educated, financially independent or endowed with family and friends who might secure them salaried positions or other "grants-in-aid" to finance their embarkation upon literary careers. Dreiser possessed none of the usual aids to a writer's career: no money, no friends in power, no formal education worthy of the name, no family tradition in letters. Still, with every disadvantage apparently massed against him, Dreiser by the force of his own will and his dogged persistence eventually burst through all barriers and produced a body of novels second to none in twentieth-century America – the very first "outsider" to break into the charmed circle of American writers.

It is useful for us to examine with some care the early life of this hulking German-American, this immigrant's son, because his life is woven so inextricably into the fabric of his novels that even a sketchy knowledge of it clarifies for the reader a good portion of the attitudes, characterizations, and prejudices that unify those books.

An American Dream Destroyed

Dreiser's German-born father, John Paul Dreiser, had entered this country some 25 years before the birth of his son Theodore in 1871 in Terre Haute, Indiana. A weaver by trade, John Paul had worked westward to establish himself and had eloped with 16-year-old Sarah Schanab,[2] daughter of a Moravian farmer living near Dayton, Ohio. The young couple moved on to Fort Wayne, where John Paul became production manager in a woolen mill, and for a time their fortunes rose. Raising enough cash to build a mill of their own, the Dreisers settled in the small town of Sullivan, where their stay was marked at first by continuing prosperity.

But in 1870 a trio of misfortunes struck. John Dreiser's woolen mill burned to the ground. During its rebuilding, a heavy beam crashed down upon the weaver's head and shoulders, destroying the hearing in one ear. While he convalesced, his guileless wife lost the remainder of the family's property. The father, according to Theodore, was broken, never the same again.

The penniless family retreated to Terre Haute, where Theodore was born the following 27 August. After him came yet another son, Edward, to complete the family. With five boys and five girls surviving infancy, it numbered an even dozen. But for the remainder of the parents' lives, the family was never again to experience the solidarity and affluence it had enjoyed so briefly in Sullivan.

"A Thin Grasshopper of a Man"

John Paul Dreiser, often incapacitated and working only sporadically, stood as a figure of grim authority, a despot, to his children. Until the novelist's later years when life had left him well-schooled "in its bitter aspects, its grim constructive process," Theodore regarded his father quite frankly as a plain fool, an ineffectual nibbler at life's banquet table, "a thin grasshopper of a man, brooding wearily."

Religious differences early built an insurmountable barrier between father and son. John Paul, though a devout and orthodox Roman Catholic, apparently neither knew nor cared greatly about his church beyond an ironclad observance of a narrow, rigid scheme of thou-shalt-nots. Following the debacle in Sullivan, he grew increasingly fanatical, obsessed "much more with the hereafter than the now." In contrast, his children, reared in poverty, deprivation, insecurity, were tantalized by the prospect of worldly pleasures – a familiar American theme. "Material possessions," reports Dreiser, "were already the goal as well as the sum of most American life, and so one could not help feeling the state of isolation and indifference which accompanied a lack of means." To the father, mindful of his obligation for the souls placed in his care by God, his children seemed much like guileless moths enticed dangerously near the fascinating lamps of corruption. He raged, threatened, and sulked, in the end creating only a deepened estrangement between him and them, a rift in the family that widened with the passing years. "Never have I known a man more obsessed by a religious belief," declares Dreiser in his autobiography; "to him God was a blazing reality." And if Dreiser's frank analysis of his family is to be given credence, the total scope of the father's moral code was limited to a set of dual emphases concerning sex and thrift.

John Paul was ever on guard to preserve his daughters' virtue, a care that was aggravated severely by the girls' own disregard for it as they bloomed into young womanhood. Very early on, they discovered men to be the most immediate source of the trinkets and flattery for which they thirsted. Inevitably the girls evaded John Paul's guard in order to go walking or buggy riding with admirers. When the father's worst fears were realized in the pregnancy of one of his daughters by a brash young local aristocrat, who promptly hopped a train for parts unknown, Dreiser's family became, as he candidly admits, "a scandal."

Not until his mature years was Dreiser capable of visualizing his father in anything other than a religious fanatic. Then the hate softened, if not to sympathy at least to pity. "How snippy and unkind I had been," he reflected, seeing his father no longer as an iron tyrant but "as he really was, warm, generous . . . a poor, tottering, broken soul wandering distrait and forlorn amid a storm of difficulties: age, the death of his wife, the flight of his children, doubt as to their salvation, poverty, a declining health." Only at the end did Dreiser award his father a due share of the compassion that he showered on most of the fictional characters he created.

"The Woman Whose Memory I Adore"

For his mother Dreiser seems to have felt only the most tender sentiments. Dreiser's numerous depictions of her show us a woman who lavished upon her many children every ounce of loving care she possessed and who provided them with whatever meager opportunities she found within her power. By nature quiet, sentimental, sympathetic, gentle – "dreamy" is the word her son most often chooses to describe her – she apparently was endowed with endless strength and patience; her enthusiasm for life faltered only when black clouds of poverty dimmed her family's prospects to the point of hopelessness. Afflicted through most of his life with a painful sense of inferiority and rejection, Dreiser confessed, "No one ever wanted me enough, unless it was my mother." In return, he bound himself tenaciously to "the silver tether of affection, understanding, sweetness, sacrifice" that she represented.

Eager to be helpful, Sarah Dreiser was not bound, as the father was, by moral codes. As a result, she stood ready to comfort and encourage any child with whom the father was angry. Did one of the restless girls hope to avert her father's wrath by meeting a current beau "on the sly"? Then the mother could be relied on to help arrange a rendezvous. Did brother Rome, "the family Nemesis," return unheralded from vagabonding it in Michigan, Kansas, Canada? Then the mother was prepared to forgive. Did "Dorsch" – as Theodore was sometimes known at home – feel the tug of the great magnet, Chicago, and burn to make his own way in the world? Then the mother stood waiting with her blessing and a few dollars scraped from her savings. Sarah Dreiser seems to have drawn her children close to her as powerfully as the father repelled them. For years after she died Dreiser felt like "a lone barque on a lone sea."

On the Move

The father's stern religiosity, the mother's flowing tenderness, the family's unceasing poverty – this trio of forces worked at shaping the young Dreiser. The lessons of life were elemental. To be poor was to be isolated, ignored, helpless. To be destitute in winter was a threat to survival itself. Food, shelter, heat, heavy clothing to cope with biting Midwestern cold: these were the needs. Money, or lack of it, was the key. Each year, even in his maturity, the advent of winter caused Dreiser to shudder with "an indefinable and highly oppressive dread." He could not witness crowded tenements in cheap, mean streets, could not see poorly clothed children, men, or women, with grimy hands and faces, without an involuntary reversion to these early and bitter memories and the wish that life "would not permit the untrained or the inadequate to stew so persistently and helplessly in their own misery."

A bewildering succession of moves and separations produced a family whose character Dreiser recognized as "nebulous, emotional, unorganized and traditionless." In Terre Haute alone the Dreisers resided in at least five or six houses, each inferior to the one before. Regularly the mother, in a burst of ambition, opened a boarding-house, and just as regularly each new venture failed. Whenever John Paul was thrown out of work, the mother would take in washing or go out to work as a scrubwoman. So desperate grew the family's situation at times during the 1870s that the younger of the 10 Dreiser children might be observed gleaning lumps of coal that had dropped on the ground along the railroad tracks. Theodore, "a most curious-minded child," was also stockpiling memories that would one day be utilized fictionally.

By 1879, the family understood that survival depended upon their splitting up. Never again would they form a truly coherent unit. The oldest girls, Mame, Emma, Theresa, and Sylvia, remained with their father on the assumption they could find work as governesses, waitresses, or clerks in five-and-ten-cent stores. The younger children, Tillie, Theodore, and Edward, accompanied the mother to Vincennes, Indiana, where a friend had offered shelter. Al was packed off to his mother's half-sister at North Manchester. Talented Paul, the oldest boy, had already struck out on his own as an apprentice in the minstrel shows so popular in that period. Rome, the next in line, had vanished for the time being to seek his fortune as a railway "candy butcher."

This painful fragmentation once agreed upon, Sarah Dreiser's optimism came springing back to its natural level. She dreamed of creating a new, more fruitful life for her children. Her friend, wife of the Vincennes firechief, lodged the group in quarters over the fire-house; and all seemed well until it dawned on Sarah that other sections of the building were being used as a brothel. Filled for once with moral indignation, Sarah herded her children back to Sullivan, where Theodore spent what he afterward considered the three happiest years of his life, "compounded of innocence, wonder, beauty, little or no trace of knowledge of good and evil or the broodings thereby entailed."

Meanwhile, the family finances had not improved. The girls in Terre Haute found life under their father's vigilant eye too restrictive. One later confided to her brother that her primary interests then were "clothes and men!" The third winter spent in Sullivan, "this worst of all winters" as Dreiser afterward recalled it, was one of utter destitution. Another attempt at running a boardinghouse had failed, draining the mother of hope. Then, with the irruptive impact of a deus ex machina, brother Paul returned after a four-year absence, splendidly clothed, already acquiring the Falstaffian corpulence that to the family was a legitimate hallmark of affluence. Paul for some time had been writing the comic and sentimental tunes that would make his fame *(On the Banks of the Wabash, My Gal Sal, I Know It's True for My Mother Told Me So)*. Having "Americanized" his name for show-business purposes, he carried with him copies of his *Paul Dresser Songbook.*

Paul's jovial, generous, reassuring presence intervened at this time to lift the gloom from his mother and to revitalize her faith in life. His well-fed, well-garbed appearance stirred in Theodore a "conception of a fate or fortune in the affairs of men – an interfering hand that beyond our understanding or willing makes or mars our inconceivably petty lives." This concept finds expression throughout Dreiser's novels, in which coincidence often is allowed to play a decisive role in human fate.

Best of all, the mother and children were taken by Paul to Evansville to the finest house they had occupied thus far. Paul forsook the vaudeville circuit temporarily to become star comedian at the Apollo Theatre, a decision prompted only in part by concern for his family, since he had fallen in love with Annie Brace, mistress of an Evansville house of prostitution. Young Theodore was unconcerned with the morality of the alliance. He knew only that Paul had acted magnanimously, had come to his mother's rescue when she most needed help. So the incident simply merged with many other observations, all of which seemed to prove the impossibility of ever defining clear-cut areas of good and evil in human affairs.

From this blurring of conventional distinctions, it was an easy leap to become fully convinced of the stupidity of all established moral codes. These, from an early age, Dreiser considered "a curse to the individual." As for ethics, they "were being taught me by life itself." What need for school or book to teach the individual about the way life organized itself in social patterns? Did one not possess eyes and ears for that purpose? Direct observation of life itself was what was called for. Enduring lessons stood ready to be learned from "the open forge and the potter's window."

"Hail, Chicago!"

Then, as suddenly as he had appeared, Paul decamped as a result of a lovers' quarrel with Annie Brace. The family regrouped, this time turning to Chicago, familiar territory to the older children and much talked up by them as the spot to relocate.

For years the magic name of Chicago had dinned Dreiser's brain. Brother Rome, brother Paul, his sisters: all who saw Chicago returned with exciting tales of that burgeoning midwestern mecca. Taut with wonder and anticipation, Dreiser was never to forget this journey. Again and again in his stories he depicts the first entry of a young American into Chicago; each newcomer is imbued with the same ecstatic thrill. "Would that I might sense it all again," Theodore exclaimed in *Dawn*, "the throb and urge and sting of my first days in Chicago!" For him nothing could ever displace as an American symbol the young Chicago, that lusty, brawling "city of big shoulders" that Carl Sandburg was soon to celebrate in verse as new and raw as the metropolis itself.

To prepare the way, three sisters preceded the family, obtained employment, and rented a six-room, third-floor apartment overlooking the Waverly Theater on West Madison. Then the mother was sent for, with the younger children. Under a plan calling for all able-bodied members to secure work and contribute to the family's support, Theodore, an impressionable twelve, became cashboy in a West Side dry goods store and later peddled newspapers on a street corner. All money was to be pooled in a common fund, with a donation from Paul taking up any slack. But well-conceived as it seemed to be, this plan was to work no better than the others. The father, thrown out of a job in Terre Haute, arrived in Chicago and reasserted his authority. Inevitably, he created discord. Having tasted freedom, the children now submitted to his restraints only under duress. Those nearing adulthood objected to contributing toward a home in which they felt unduly shackled. Dissension followed speedily, and in the end nothing was possible but still another move, this time to Warsaw, Indiana. There was no choice. The father returned to Terre Haute with plans to rejoin the family later in Warsaw; the older children clung to their Chicago positions; the mother, with her younger brood, left for Indiana.

"The Charm of Warsaw"

Now the story repeated itself – this time with more dire conse-
quences. Rome returned, shaming the family again with his delin-
quency. Next came the father. Following him, two sisters, "a vivid,
harum-scarum pair." "Such a bold, shameless way to dress!" the
father raged when he discovered them with lips and cheeks rouged,
spit curls plastered to their cheeks, and gowned in "borrowed
finery." One of the girls returned to Chicago and then married a
Tammany Hall politician, but the other remained in Warsaw, only to
become pregnant by the son of a leading family in town. The wagging
of local tongues over this scandal left an indelible impression on
Theodore, driving home strongly "the chill resentment . . . the
sudden whispers, evasions, desires to avoid those who have failed to
conform to the customs and taboos of any given region!" His notions
of the incontestable power of society over the individual were
beginning to jell.

Young Dreiser had observed with great wonder and considerable dismay the powerful manner in which the sexual drive influenced his sisters' behavior and determined their fates. Now it
entered his own life, awakening in his adolescent body like a "hot
fire nature had lighted." More and more it occupied his thoughts,
filling his dreams with conquests of love. More affluent boys he
envied hotly for their handsome appearances, their splendid clothes,
for what he took to be their courage. As for the Warsaw girls, they
surrounded him with a "stinging richness" so far beyond his grasp
that day and night he felt himself tantalized by delights he might
never have the force to possess.

To one in Dreiser's position – penniless, inexperienced, eternally an outsider – desirable girls seemed more unattainable than
stars. For years to come, he dreamed impossible dreams of himself as
the central actor in a perfect love affair. He craved always to "shine
as a lover," and his later notorious promiscuity (which he liked to
call "varietism") might be traced to this source.[3] "Sex," he admits
with his characteristic candor, "harried me from hell to hell!"

At the same time, much of life in the village of Warsaw was
rewarding. In his spare time Dreiser was reading voraciously, albeit
hampered by being able to use only his left eye, the right having a
cast. The magic of the printed page put him under a spell. "Books!

Books! Books! How wonderful, fascinating, revealing!"[4] Hawthorne's
The House of the Seven Gables and Kingsley's *Water Babies* attracted
him in particular; thoughts of the latter always recalled for him those
happy days when, as a young lad, he had explored "pools and
waterholes watching for crawfish and salamanders." He immersed
himself in Dickens, then in Thackeray; read widely in Shakespeare;
tasted Bunyan, Fielding, Pope, Thoreau, Emerson, Twain; and tried
history. But his true literary influences, such as Balzac, lay waiting to
be discovered.

Life for a time seemed "lush, full and sweet, a veritable youth-
dream of lotus land." Warsaw stood at the beginning of a chain of
small lakes extending for 30 miles eastward, and this uninhabited
country allowed him to walk alone for hours at a time while thinking
– sometimes brooding – but also continually delighted by the natural spectacle.

Best of all, Dreiser was enrolled in a school he enjoyed, and he
had found a teacher who understood him. Mildred Fielding,
gracious, sympathetic – rather like his own mother in temperament
– recognized in this awkward, self-conscious youth something of
herself as a young girl and went out of her way to praise his reading
and composition, to comment favorably on his mental abilities.
Gradually, Theodore came to feel he might perhaps be of some
worth after all.

But with school dismissed for the summer, Theodore felt a latent
wanderlust welling up in him. Chicago! Sixteen now, he was chafing
to stamp his mark on the world. Never mind that he was inexperienced, poorly endowed physically and psychologically, not only
painfully aware of all his inadequacies, but prone to magnifying
them; even so, his spirit welled over with blind confidence. He went
into the house. "Ma," he announced, "I am going to Chicago." With
tears in her eyes, Sarah Dreiser scraped together $6 for him – the
train fare took $1.75 of it – and he hustled to pack his bag for the
"most intense and wonderful" trip of his life.

Surely, argued the boy, somewhere in the teeming activity of
Chicago there must be a place for an ambitious youth like himself.
The American Dream had taken such strong possession of him that it
came as a rude shock to find no doors swinging open to welcome his
presence. Disenchanted, the boy dropped his sights considerably,
applying wherever he might as common labor. Even here he discov-

ered himself at a disadvantage competing with young fellows who were toughened by schooling in the city streets. Eventually he did find employment – as a dishwasher in a fly-specked restaurant. Seething with the conviction that such labor demeaned him, he quit the moment he located a job with Hibbard, Spencer, Bartlett and Company, a large wholesale hardware store. But working there turned out to be not much more rewarding and the new job only confused and embittered him further.

More forcibly than ever before, Dreiser discovered "the luck of being born rich . . . the insufferable difference between wealth and poverty." Contrast, he saw, was what drilled one in learning how life organized itself. "Differences present life's edge and give it its zest," he realized. "We enjoy or disdain what we have because of contrast with what we do or do not have, what we do or do not endure." A series of novels would dramatize that principle. Carrie Meeber, Jennie Gerhardt, Clyde Griffiths – these protagonists all learn the realities of life in America by observing, as Dreiser had, the explicit signs of the contrasts between affluence and poverty.

"One Dreamy, Lackadaisical Year"

At the very moment when it appeared morbidly possible to Dreiser that he might have doomed himself to life as a "commonplace" hardware stock boy, another of life's inexplicable strokes of chance steered his fortunes upward. Miss Fielding, who had left Warsaw after teaching Theodore in his first high school year, found him in Chicago. Believing in the young man's potential, she outlined a plan that would send him to college – a year, perhaps two – at her expense.

In the fall of 1889, Dreiser enrolled at Indiana University, and for the first time in his life enjoyed a sense of genuine importance. Well aware of his good fortune, he knew intuitively that he stood at one of life's crossroads. But even so, college never became for him the catalytic experience that he assumed and that Miss Fielding hoped it might prove to be; for, without being altogether conscious of it, he had long ago chanced upon his proper method for learning. Life itself had become his schoolroom and refused to be supplanted. Books might prove of value, but they would never supersede in importance the direct observation that had already taught young

Dreiser so much about the human struggle. As for his academic year spent in Bloomington, he later revealed that "its technical educational value to me was zero."

In Bloomington Dreiser was struck again by the unfair contrasts that characterized life. Especially, he perceived these inequities embodied in his roommate, who seemed so handsome, bold, magnetic. Why should this fellow be so well equipped by life, breezing into Bloomington with two trunks loaded with jackets, suits, and shoes the like of which Theodore could scarcely dream of possessing? Why was Dreiser himself so ill endowed? Why had nature showered everything on one and nothing on the other? "I used to look at him," says Dreiser, "and then at myself after he was gone and ask myself what chance had I?" Clothes made the man, it seemed. With suitable garments one might sweep through doors shut tightly against those who lacked the uniform of caste. He found no reason why a few yards of wool or silk should assume such great social importance. Yet it seemed to be so; and most of Dreiser's young fictional heroes and heroines are endowed, like their creator, with an instinctive awareness of the value of clothes as a "status-symbol."

At the end of his freshman year, when students gathered for a traditional burning of books, Dreiser, always an injustice collector, refused to attend these "silly revelries" that would serve no purpose except to remind him of "the deprivations I had endured, the things in which I had not been included, the joys which many had had and which I had not." Of those who had ignored him during his college year, he exclaimed bluntly, "They can all go to hell!"

He left Bloomington never to return.

"A Lone Barque on a Lone Sea"

Dreiser came back to Chicago determined to keep his sights set above the menial labor that had heretofore been his lot. Noting the city's rapid expansion into the suburbs, he went to work as a salesman in a real-estate office, a position that promised high commissions that never materialized. But this disappointment paled beside the critical illness of Sarah Dreiser in August 1889. For weeks "the central centripetal star" of Dreiser's life declined, and finally all members of the scattered family who could be contacted were called home to say their farewells.

On a day in November, while Theodore was helping his mother to the toilet, she sagged in his arms, gave him "a most exhausted and worn look," and died. "Oh, I should have gone first!" cried the father, forlorn and exhausted. And Dreiser himself, rather bitterly, echoed in his thoughts, "Yes, why not?" But it was brother Al who spoke most pertinently. "Well," he told the rest of the clan, "that's the end of our home."

Al was correct. Within a year most of the children had deserted their father; and Theodore found himself completely on his own, a rudderless ship without compass, sextant, or anchor. At $8.00 a week, he drove a delivery wagon for Munger's Laundry, a job that gave him entry into homes ranging from the crudest tenement and "bed house" to opulent apartments of fabulously wealthy capitalists. He was quick to notice that the type of reception a laundryman received corresponded scarcely at all with the economic levels of the persons he dealt with. Rich and poor were equally likely to insult him as a lackey or to respect him as a human individual. He began to develop a "fairly clear perception of the value of personality as distinct from either poverty or riches." After all, he reasoned, who could have been consistently more destitute than his own mother? Yet poverty had never altered her importance to him.

The poor, he was beginning to see more clearly, were not necessarily virtuous, nor were the wealthy altogether diabolical. All human creatures seemed to be trapped in somewhat the same nets. People seemed to be little more than bits of seaweed on an endless ocean, swept this way and that by submarine tides of chance and circumstance that they neither controlled nor understood. They were puppets, toys. "But where," he questioned, "is the toy-maker who makes us?"

Dreiser's mind echoed with its constant refrain: "No common man am I." His eyes were fixed upon the "real rulers of the world" – bankers, millionaires, artists, executives; fame and wealth stirred him "like whips and goads." He was no common man, to be sure – but how best could he achieve uncommon status? It was during this period of decision that Dreiser first began thinking, albeit in vague, dreamlike terms, of becoming a writer. "It would be a wonderful thing to be a novelist," he thought. Such a notion is not uncommon to perceptive youths who dream of fame through accomplishment. For most the dream remains frozen in the snowpack of fantasy. For

Dreiser, the dream was eventually to come true, though a decade and more would pass first.

Newspaper Days

Young Dreiser took stock of himself.[5] The possibility of his acquiring sudden wealth by any means was quite obviously out of the question. Few young Americans of his acquaintance, portrayals in popular dime novels notwithstanding, seemed to be getting ahead by marrying their bosses' daughters. The prospect of emerging as a prominent novelist overnight was equally discouraging. But perhaps he could make a beginning at least by placing himself with one of Chicago's newspapers. Determined to force his way upward, at age 21 he set out to bedazzle the local editors. For weeks a brusque "Nothing today!" iced down every flush of hope; but at last John Maxwell, copyreader of the city's lowest-ranking newspaper, the *Daily Globe*, accepted Theodore on a trial basis. After that his imaginative coverage of the 1892 Democratic convention won him a chance at a steady berth and for the next decade he was occupied primarily in journalistic work: reporting, editing, publishing scores of feature articles in the popular magazines.

The newspaper world fell a good distance short of the nirvana Dreiser had imagined it to be. Always a bit naive, the man often was taken aback when his dream bubbles burst in the nippy air of reality. Only his great and wonderful illusion of Chicago remained undimmed: with her impressive new skyscrapers, her tall grain elevators, immense railroad yards, imposing mansions, teeming slum areas, the city was for Dreiser a "whirlpool of life." But the longer he dwelt in the newspaper world, the more he found the struggle for survival to be a fierce battle in which the motive of self-interest predominated. Journalism revealed itself to be a smaller representation of life's larger image, a more distinctly outlined universe perhaps. But one that otherwise seemed identical in character to all he had observed elsewhere. But he had cast his lot with the newspaper business, and, offered a job on the Saint Louis *Globe-Democrat*, he left Chicago. It was not an easy decision, but it seemed an essential one if he were to rise in the world.

Throughout his newspaper career, Dreiser always was struck forcefully by the contrast between the truth of life as he daily observed it and the all-too-often cheating illusion of life he was commanded to report in his articles. Rarely did truth and illusion seem to coincide. Journalism, as he experienced it, was dominated by a "sweetness and light code" that presented the world as a never-never land in which sin and shame were reserved exclusively for outcasts, criminals, and vagrants. This distorted representation of life he considered to be diametrically opposed to everything he had witnessed since infancy: "All men were honest – only they weren't; all women were virtuous and without evil intent or design – but they weren't; all mothers were gentle, self-sacrificing slaves, sweet pictures for song and Sunday Schools – only they weren't; all fathers were kind, affectionate, saving, industrious – only they weren't. But when describing actual facts for the news columns, you were not allowed to indicate these things."[6] "What a howl," he concluded, would arise should a reporter portray in story or novel a genuinely true and realistic image of life in America drawn solely from his daily observations!

Now to Saint Louis came Paul Dresser, traveling with a melodrama entitled *The Danger Signal.* The two brothers met for serious talk. What was Theodore doing in Saint Louis? asked the elder. New York – that was the only place for a young man of ambition and talent, the one city where men of promise might hope to attain their full intellectual stature. Paul's representation of New York as the beating heart of the nation's artistic and business life took root. Before long Theodore junked his Saint Louis career to set out for the East, working briefly along the way for newspapers in Toledo, Cleveland, Buffalo, Pittsburgh.

Each city provided experiences that further crystallized Dreiser's maturing social views. In Toledo, a streetcar strike was in progress. Without previous knowledge of the case, he leaped intuitively to the workers' defense: "I had seen enough of strikes, and of poverty, and of the quarrels between the money-lords and the poor, to be all on one side." He stored away his memories of the strike; later, he siphoned them fresh and clear from his memory when writing of Hurstwood's decline in *Sister Carrie.*

In Buffalo, and particularly in Pittsburgh, Dreiser witnessed late nineteenth-century industrial America at its most lawless and savage. The city bred multimillionaires: "On every hand were giants plotting, fighting, dreaming." And in contrast to the mansions of these titans were the most squalid slums he had ever witnessed. How was it, he pondered, that some men might soar the heavens like eagles, while others, sparrows, were permitted to flit about on the lower levels only?

The paradox of wealth and poverty was apparent everywhere – but might not be written about. Dreiser's editor on the Pittsburgh *Dispatch,* fully aware of which side his bread was buttered on, cautioned emphatically, "Don't touch on labor problems." Anything regarding the city's industrial demigods or its festering social issues was to be handled gingerly, if at all. "We don't touch on scandals in high life. The big steel men here just about own the place, so we can't . . . We have to be mighty careful what we say" (*Myself,* 406).

Commented young Dreiser, "So much for a free press in Pittsburgh, A.D. 1893!"

A Storm-breeding Mistake

It had been winter when Dreiser left Missouri. Now spring had given way to summer. Five months of wandering – Toledo, Cleveland, Buffalo, Pittsburgh – a few weeks here, a month there. And though the odyssey had been of greater value than he could then know, Dreiser was alone, unsure of his direction, and dismayed at his apparent lack of progress. Moreover, he was 21 years old and in love, caught in the grip of a "chemism" he could neither comprehend nor control.

Dreiser had first met Sara White during the previous summer when the Saint Louis *Republic,* to boost its circulation, promoted a "popularity contest" to determine Missouri's favorite schoolmarms. The prize was a trip to the 1892 Chicago World's Fair. Dreiser, because of his Chicago connections, had been assigned to accompany the all-state winners and their chaperones in a private Pullman car, to escort them on a tour of the fairgrounds, and to make journalistic capital of their trip by sending back feature articles.

Once aboard the train, he found it hard to avert his eyes from one beauty in particular: "She was in white, with a mass of sunny red hair. Her eyes were almond-shaped, liquid and blue-grey. Her nose was straight and fine, her lips sweetly curved. She seemed bashful and retiring. At her bosom was a bouquet of pink roses" (*Myself,* 240).

In the days following, as he squired Sara White beside the blue lagoons and snowy white buildings of the World's Fair or escaped alone with her to view such Chicago showplaces as the colored fountain erected in Lincoln Park by Charles T. Yerkes, the philanthropist-financier,[7] Theodore perceived in his new fascination a host of virtues. The girl appeared to have everything: humor, romance, understanding, patience, sympathy, the very qualities he most required. Their days in Chicago passed in a euphoria of sightseeing, hand-holding, and tender sentiments. A good deal more than a holiday romance was in the making; it was love, no doubt about it; and Dreiser did not descend to earth until it was too late. Marriage was not really what he craved at all, but possession. His "peculiarly erratic and individual" personality prized its freedom above all else, and marriage could only lock him in chains that sooner or later would require breaking. It is ironic and deeply unfortunate that the rigidly conventional Sara White should have become the object of Dreiser's desire. One life, one love – this was her ideal. First the wooing, then the wedding, was the pattern she clung to. Two young people more differently constituted would be difficult to imagine. On one level Dreiser realized this truth, or had strong inklings of it, but he did not realize it fully enough to dispel the perfumed veils of illusion that hovered about his head like mists on a mountaintop, fogging his vision. "I was as much a victim of passion and romance as she was," he afterward recollected, "only to the two of us it did not mean the same thing."

Five years later, having corresponded sporadically with her and wrestled mentally with his own disoriented emotions, Dreiser sent for Sara White, married her in Washington, and brought her to New York as his wife. To Dreiser, this ill-starred marriage would afterward stand as a sign of the overpowering chemical attractions that govern human actions and through which nature manages always to have her way. The catastrophe was a bitter experience that would find its way to the center of a number of novels and stories, although in later years Dreiser would wax philosophic about:

As I look back on it I can imagine no greater error of mind or temperament than that which drew me to her, considering my own variable tendencies and my naturally freedom-loving point of view. But since we are all blind victims of chance and given to far better hind-sight than fore-sight I have no complaint. It is quite possible that this was all a part of my essential destiny of development, one of those storm-breeding mistakes by which one grows. Life seems thus often casually to thrust upon one an experience which is to prove illuminating or disastrous. (*Myself,* 260)

This is not to say that the Dreiser marriage proved unhappy from the start; but even granting that both young people made an effort toward harmony, the honeymoon was brief. They were too different; they clashed on too many issues of vital importance. Theodore was an artist, or hoped to be; Sarah was a Philistine to the core. With Theodore holding to the pagan "varietism" he had long since adopted, only time staved off the inevitable clash.

Damon Meets Pythias

In his travels eastward from Missouri to New York, Dreiser had augmented his well of memory with a store of incidents and individuals who later might be tapped for fictional purposes; and he had stumbled on at least one enduring and influential friendship. The young editor in Toledo who had hired him for four days' writing, including coverage of a streetcar strike, proved to have a personality so compatible with Dreiser's that Dreiser was led to confess, "If he had been a girl I would have married him." Like Dreiser, Arthur Henry harbored literary ambitions. The two men stepped out to lunch, and so intense was their "varied and gay exchange of intimacies" that they did not return to the office for three hours. They talked and talked and talked, two young men of intellectual affinity, facing each other as equals. Here at last was someone with whom serious intellectual and literary conversation might be held on some basis other than editor to cub or old hand to neophyte. Youth spoke to youth, ambition to ambition. A newspaper post in Toledo failing to materialize, Dreiser continued on to New York. Establishing himself in the great metropolis was not easy. It was a shock to discover that in New York a newcomer could not get so much as a peek at a city editor, the sanctum sanctorum of such a worthy being watchdogged by "supercilious, scoffing" anteroom sentinels.

Dreiser was elated when at last he was taken on the staff of Pulitzer's *World,* but his euphoria thinned considerably upon discovering that he was to be hired on "space," meaning that he would in a sense free-lance and be paid by the column for whatever of his reporting the paper chose to purchase. Depressing as such an appointment was – sometimes the results of his day's work scarcely covered his car fare – the assignments carried him to every corner of the city: the East Side, the Bowery, the Brooklyn waterfront, Wall Street, the Tenderloin, Fifth Avenue. The contrasts of life he had observed in Chicago and the steel cities paled beside the greater spectacle of New York. Everywhere his observations of city life were identical: "Either a terrifying desire for lust or pleasure or wealth, accompanied by a heartlessness which was freezing to the soul, or a dogged resignation to deprivation and misery." There seemed, in all of America, no escape from this pattern.

Now, for the first time, Dreiser began to consider the possibility of writing fiction, short stories perhaps. Time was not inuring him to the frustrations of newspaper work. He felt a nagging and even insistent stimulus to set down on paper some of his honest observations and conclusions about life, not as they had to be muted in order to appease the timid public press but as he genuinely felt them. But who would publish such outspoken material? Could he possibly be wrong about life? Was it actually as bright and optimistic, as neat and laden with ideals as so many of the magazine writers insisted? He was sure it was not. His experience told him otherwise. Stronger and stronger grew the need to abandon journalism entirely, to strike out on his own. If he failed, he would have the satisfaction of having failed on his own terms; if he succeeded, he might reap the rewards.

Brother Paul came to the rescue now as dependably as he had in the past. When Paul's sheet-music publishers established a new music periodical, *Ev'ry Month,* Theodore was made editor. Among the contributors, very soon, was – no surprise – Arthur Henry of Toledo. Renewing his acquaintance with Dreiser, Henry nagged him to try his hand at fiction, inviting him on a number of occasions to come and stay at his own home in Ohio if time and solitude were what was required.

The invitation appealed strongly to Dreiser; yet it was not possible to accept until 1899, when he and Sara traveled to Ohio to spend the summer with the Henrys, who occupied a large white Greek revival home overlooking the Maumee River near Toledo. In this idyllic vacation atmosphere the two men, working together, acted as catalysts upon each other, stimulating, criticizing, and praising when praise seemed deserved. Under Henry's prodding, Dreiser initiated a series of short stories and before long was gratified to have some of them accepted for publication. The first, "The Shining Slave Makers,"[8] fittingly portrayed the jungle world of two rival ant colonies involved in bloody conflict to the death. In its demonstration of "nature red in tooth and claw" and of the preservation of the mass at the expense of the individual, it developed a theme Dreiser would handle on innumerable later occasions. Invariably he took his stand with the individual in protesting what seemed nature's unjust method for advancing the species. Soon followed "The Door of the Butcher Rogaum" and "Nigger Jeff,"[9] both based upon incidents observed during his newspaper stint in Saint Louis.

Arthur Henry, eagerly beginning work on his novel, *A Princess of Arcady,* urged Dreiser to try a book-length work of fiction. As Dreiser put it, "He began to ding-dong about a novel. I must write a novel. I must write a novel." And pat as the story sounds, Dreiser insists that to please his friend he sat down one day in September and, choosing a title at random, wrote on a yellow sheet of paper the words *Sister Carrie* – thus turning a new page in American literary history.[10]

Chapter Two

"A Waif amid Forces":
Sister Carrie

The Mechanism Called Man

By that summer of 1899 when at age 28 he began his first novel, Theodore Dreiser had matured substantially into the man he was to remain for the rest of his life. Having observed life at first hand with the eagerness of a young biologist, Dreiser, like Henry David Thoreau, had driven life into a corner, reduced it to its lowest terms, and confronted its essential facts – both of meanness and of sublimity. But, unlike Thoreau, he saw meanness as prevailing in men's lives; sublimity, if it existed at all, hovered like a range of delectable mountains somewhere beyond the horizon and nearly unattainable.

Without ever substantially altering his theories, Dreiser would, decade after decade, book upon book, publish to the world his finding that life at bottom was a tragedy. Life was inexplicable, of course. This granted, it was gigantic, overpowering, a dizzying, furious mélange emerging apparently from nowhere, headed nowhere. Life had much to do with "chemisms" and "magnetisms"; it was dominated by invincible material forces; and of these the drives for power, money, and sex were primary. Man seemed to be little more than the puppet of such forces, a mere wisp in the wind (as Dreiser put it in *Sister Carrie*), a leaf on the maelstrom that through sheer accident, good luck or bad, cast a few up and many down. In the process, life produced wild and undeserved extremes of fortune.

Dreiser could not have known it in 1899, but in beginning *Sister Carrie* he was launching himself upon a long career that would ultimately make him the most significant of American writers of the school later known as literary naturalism. As a genre, naturalism had begun during the 1880s in France with the writer Emile Zola, whose book *The Naturalistic Novel* had named and defined it. Except for a very few, American writers during the 1890s remained unaware of Zola's work. But Stephen Crane had followed his principles, and Frank Norris studied Zola intently and in *McTeague* (1899) produced the first truly naturalistic novel in America. As both Crane and Norris died young, it remained for Dreiser to carry on what they had begun.

Precisely what naturalism was (or is) is not always a simple task to explain. For Zola, it was a fictional view of life that allied itself closely to the scientific movement. He envisioned novels as akin to "laboratory experiments," conducted by writers of great objectivity; life itself – society – was the laboratory in which writers would find ready-made plots that could be duplicated in fiction by way of close observation and a massing of supportive detail. With life supplying the plots, novels would become "reports" on the novelists' findings.

Dreiser, of course, thought of himself as a realist, then the accepted term for writers who leaned more on actuality than imagination and for whom the quest for truth was paramount. But when he insisted that in *Sister Carrie* his major attempt had been to provide "a picture of conditions" prevailing in the American life of his times, he was verging closely upon the aims Zola had advocated.

In the historical background that led to literary naturalism, the evolutionary theories of Charles Darwin were extremely important, but Dreiser was influenced more directly by an English contemporary of Darwin, Herbert Spencer, whose book *First Principles* was first published in America during the 1880s and was read by Dreiser while he was a young newspaperman in Pittsburgh. Like Darwin a champion of the evolutionary principle, Spencer presented a persuasive image of man standing alone and fragile, at the mercy of immense universal forces that he could neither understand nor control. Spencer's materialist philosophy suited an age already dominated by scientific thought. All phenomena were to be classified as either knowable or unknowable. Declaring the pursuit of the unknowable as inappropriate for finite human minds, Spencer emphasized the propriety of examining the knowable – in Dreiser's case, the facts of the life and society in which he lived.

For Spencer, the concept of religion, with its claim to revealed truth and its ultimate assumption of self-existence, was an element of the unknowable and thus to be discarded. This was a position that the already skeptical young Dreiser was eager to accept. Other fundamentals of Spencer's scheme became familiar elements in Dreiser's thought, particularly the idea that the universe was controlled by irresistible forces acting upon matter and mind to determine events in the phenomenological world. Evolution – merely another name for life, the unending process of change and development – was for Spencer the product of these same persistent forces. The forces themselves defied understanding, although humanity might perceive them at work through their manifestations in society. Space and time were equally incomprehensible, matter no less so, the idea of motion illusory, the exercise of force wholly unintelligible. Even the existence of the individual personality was by no means to be thought of as being established as fact. The greatest, the ultimate truth was that nothing finally can be known for certain.

The effect of Spencer's ideas was shattering: Dreiser openly acknowledged that they blew him to bits intellectually, driving out of his mind whatever idealistic tendencies he had entertained and confirming the most pessimistic fears that his observations had suggested. In the burgeoning industrial world in which he found himself, a brutal individualistic spirit appeared to dominate, a spirit much akin to that which was central in Darwin's world of the jungle where "kill or be killed" was the law, survival of the fittest the aim. In society these principles appeared to be no less dominant. Endowed by heredity with the right qualities, a man might for a time become a commanding figure, even a millionaire. But in that same capricious world he might just as easily end as a derelict in a bread-line, commit suicide, and have his corpse be consigned to potter's field. In his novels Dreiser described both extremes, expressing deep compassion for victors and vanquished alike – because in life there were no final winners. Death came as the end to all endeavors. It was a frightening challenge, this new freedom to succeed mightily – or to fail. When the human individual was placed in such straits, the primacy of self-interest was clearly indicated, and most of Dreiser's characters are – like Carrie Meeber – kept too busy looking out for their own survival to worry much about becoming their brother's keeper.

Literary naturalism as it grew during Dreiser's lifetime emphasized certain common traits. It portrayed heredity and environment as important deterministic forces shaping highly individualized characters presented in special, heavily detailed circumstances. These forces were joined by an intense interest in the impact of psychology, sometimes to the point of blurring the distinction between the novel and the scientific case study. At bottom life was shown to be ironic, even tragic. The concept of nature as existing in a benign relationship with man was replaced by a sense of nature as indifferent and even hostile to human hopes and aspirations. In this portrait, the human being was reduced from a commanding position to a position of ultimate powerlessness both in the social scheme and in the universal pattern. These ideas were shared by many writers, yet each naturalist was different from the other, especially in emphasis. For Dreiser the large question of life's import itself became a central feature of all his fiction. Asked during his middle years for a statement of his life philosophy, he described earthly existence as "a welter of inscrutable forces" in which was trapped each "utterly infinitesimal" human being: "I catch no meaning from all I have seen, and pass quite as I came, confused and dismayed."

If the weird formula called life could not easily be defined, it could be described. And this, beginning with *Sister Carrie,* is what Dreiser set himself to do. His first novel would describe American values for what he had found them to be – materialistic to the core. The money ideal would be exposed as the great motivating purpose of life in the United States, where one's affluence determined the degree of creature comfort one might enjoy, the measure of prestige one might claim, the extent of social power one might command. In all of *Sister Carrie* there is not one character whose status is not determined economically. Individuals claw their way upward, consuming conspicuously along the trail, rising by means fair or foul. One summit is reached only to reveal another, loftier, more magnetic in appeal. And so life passes in a meaningless quest for a kind of El Dorado, in perennial dissatisfaction. Bliss lies eternally just one more easy step ahead, "up there" where homes are more palatial, clothes more splendid, carriages more sumptuous.

These things *Sister Carrie* says about America in a loud, clear voice; and by saying them in 1900 its author could scarcely be courting popularity. Once it was published, a few perceptive critics praised Dreiser's novel; some solid citizens were shocked or pretended to be shocked by it. Dreiser's own publisher did his best to smother it. But the novel has survived to become an American classic.

A Young Girl's Odyssey

The basic story of *Sister Carrie* is uncomplicated.[1] Three human leaves are caught in the winds of chance and circumstance. One is tossed upward toward (but never reaching) fulfillment, another is dragged downward to ruin, a third is swept along briskly but at a dead level. Of Dreiser's principals, Carrie Meeber begins as an 18-year-old "waif amid forces" and ends as Carrie Madenda, popular favorite of the musical comedy stage. George Hurstwood we meet as the impeccably groomed manager of a prosperous Chicago saloon but leave as a ragged, penniless suicide in New York. Charles Drouet, the single minor character whose career the novel spans, both begins and ends as a shallow but congenial salesman, a personality boy; he is so steadily prosperous that he never consciously confronts the forces that shape him.

In 1889, on an afternoon in August, Caroline Meeber, unencumbered by moral values but "full of the illusions of ignorance and youth," boards the Chicago train in Columbia City, Wisconsin. She possesses her train ticket, $4 in a yellow leather snap purse, and no idea at all of what she may find to do in the city. What happens to a young girl of this type under these circumstances? In the Dreiserian world, she will fall under the sway of the "forces wholly superhuman" that govern life. Her overweening drive for self-interest will motivate her in every instance. Her rise will depend upon her ability to resist any distraction from the main chance. Finally, her success or failure will be determined by the good or bad luck that chance metes out and by her innate adaptability to new circumstances.

On the train into Chicago, an hour has not passed before Carrie is reacting to these dark, mysterious forces. From the seat behind her, flashy Charles Drouet initiates a conversation, and although "a certain sense of what was conventional" warns Carrie to remain aloof, the drummer's "magnetism" prevails. Impressed by his purse choked with greenbacks, his new suit and shiny tan shoes, and his general sheen of sophistication, Carrie soon is speaking with Drouet as confidentially as if he were an old family friend.

This readiness to respond to advances made by a stranger on a train contravenes the accepted mores of behavior for young ladies in 1889, but Carrie's curiosity and her alert attention to the possibilities extended by life win out over any cautionary training she may have received from her parents. Upon reaching the railroad depot in Chicago, Carrie adapts once again to the ruling social circumstance. Expecting her married sister, Minnie Hanson, to meet her, she reverts to accepted patterns of behavior and makes certain that Minnie will not see her in close company with the stranger Drouet. Yet a tacit understanding has been established between Carrie and Drouet that they may well meet again, as they do, without Minnie being aware of it. In separating herself from Drouet at the depot, Carrie handily forestalls any embarrassing questions regarding the acceptability of her behavior. At the same time, this scene sets a pattern for the future, in which Carrie habitually leads a double life. On the surface, she follows conventional patterns. On another, more important level, she follows the dictates of her sense of self-interest as it leads her – or promises to lead her – toward desired goals. And on this level her behavior, in the social sense, is decidedly unconventional.

When Carrie arrives at her sister's meager Chicago flat, she feels "cold reality taking her by the hand." Minnie and Sven Hanson of necessity restrict their activities to the daily cycle of early rising and long, hard hours at the job of keeping body and soul together. In the immense industrial machinery of 1889 Chicago, they are but tiny, dispensable cogs. They are, in fact, counting on Carrie to help them prosper. None of these elements of the Hansons' "lean and narrow life" are lost on Carrie, who perceives instinctively the true state of affairs. Just as her brief encounter with Drouet had flashed to her a glimmer of those attractive things she must by some means acquire, she also realizes immediately that the Hansons epitomize a fate she must avoid.

Implications hint to us that Carrie has received only the most rudimentary home training in social behavior. As far as moral values are concerned, that training has no salutary effect upon her actions in the world. For all practical purposes, her mind became a tabula rasa the moment she entered the day coach to Chicago, and since then the pencil of experience has been furiously occupied in scribbling on it the lessons taken from her observations. Life's contrasts have begun their tutorial process.

A quick learner, Carrie soon knows more specifically what it is she wants: comfort, money, security. But how is she ever to achieve what seem the only worthwhile rewards in life? To an unequipped newcomer no route toward "success" appears open except perhaps that of shop girl at miserable wages. Carrie begins her round of job seeking in the intimidating brick commercial canyons of Chicago, where sleek facades of brass and plate glass bar her from golden mysteries of financial conquest. She musters her courage to apply for work, but one cold dismissal follows another. Carrie is consumed by thoughts of people "counting money, dressing magnificently, and riding in carriages." Each footsore step she takes carries her farther away from this golden vision. Craving pleasure, she is offered misery in its place.

When Carrie does locate work, it is in a shoe factory, operating a punch that cuts holes for laces; this is sweatshop labor, grueling hours without rest. Her lower-class coworkers disgust her. In their abandonment of hope she glimpses the specter of her own probable future. Worst of all, her wages amount to a scant $4.50 a week, out of which she must pay $4 board and room to her sister Minnie.

Carrie despairs when she loses her job after an illness, but by sheer coincidence she encounters Drouet on Chicago's crowded streets. Out of the sea of faces he appears, as if by magic, taking her by the arm, and ushering her into a splendid dining room for a feast. Sirloin – at $1.25 a plate! Carrie is overwhelmed. Without question she accepts a "loan" of $20, "two soft, green ten-dollar bills." All scruples are now overruled. Carrie promises to meet her Prince Charming the next morning to shop for new clothes. Because the new clothes are much too fine and expensive ever to be accounted for at home, Carrie leaves the Hansons' apartment in secrecy and moves to a room Drouet has taken for his "sister" on Wabash Street. Soon the two of them are sharing a comfortable three-room flat in Ogden Place, and Carrie is the proud possessor of all it takes, at this time, to make her happy: fine clothes, abundant money, and the attention of Drouet, who in her eyes seems the capstone of charm, elegant taste, and generosity.

But *Sister Carrie* was not to be a conventional Cinderella tale. Dreiser once considered titling his novel *The Flesh and the Spirit;* he might equally well have considered *The Unsatisfied,* which states the essence of Carrie's story. Rising to one crest of affluence she craves more, or something different. Contrasts impinge on her from all sides, stirring her to restlessness. A chance encounter on the street with girls from the shoe factory impresses her all the more with the misery she has avoided and the security of the plateau she has reached under Drouet's protection. But eventually this is precisely the thorn that rankles. It *is* a plateau, and Carrie's nature always aspires to rise.

Having taken one step up the socioeconomic ladder, Carrie is poised to climb higher. But that requires another helping hand. Dreiser now introduces into Carrie's life the figure of George Hurstwood, manager of Hannah and Hogg's elegant downtown saloon. Drouet prides himself on his friendship with Hurstwood, a man more successful, considerably more polished, "more clever than Drouet in a hundred ways," and much more affluent. Carrie, forming her judgments always upon the basis of material appearance, cannot avoid comparing the two men. Hurstwood invites Drouet and Carrie to see the famous actor Joseph Jefferson perform in *Rip Van Winkle*, and in the expensive box, surrounded by people of means, with Hurstwood affable, fluent, greatly at ease in this higher realm, it is "driven into Carrie's mind that here was the superior man. She instinctively felt that he was the stronger and higher."

Unluckily for Hurstwood, Carrie's rising esteem for him is matched on his part by infatuation. Carrie's fresh 18-year-old beauty and her deference to his station in life contrast with the shrewishness of Hurstwood's wife. His bond with Julia Hurstwood has become a marriage in name only, held together by children, money, status, and the power of social convention. And so Hurstwood, in mid-life crisis, is extremely vulnerable, despite outward appearances. Carrie attracts him powerfully and, as it will turn out, fatally. Here Dreiser begins a powerful demonstration of the overriding impact of sexual desire in life, an impact that Dreiser attributes to an indefinable but overpowering "magnetism" composed of chemical affinities integral to the powerful Spencerian forces that govern human existence and reduce the human being to an uncomprehending "wisp in the wind."

Faced with the relative mystery of why and how an untutored country girl such as Carrie could exert such a deranging power over an intelligent and worldly-wise executive such as Hurstwood, the reader must understand that such attractions occur regularly in human experience and have very little to do with logical, controlled behavior. At the same time, one must grant Carrie credit for doing what she can to suit herself for Hurstwood. Possessed of a sharp eye,

Carrie learns rapidly. From Drouet's comments concerning what he admires in other women she discovers a host of detailed refinements concerning dress and demeanor that can augment a woman's charm. Carrie's neighbor, Mrs. Hale, plays her part in opening the girl's eyes to the decorum of those towering above her on the social ladder. But even with these considerations, Hurstwood's passion is perhaps best explained by Dreiser as the irresistible allure of the flame for the moth.

From the beginning, Carrie's life is motivated by strong desires for security, for wealth (and particularly clothes, wealth's emblem), and for pleasure. The first of these she has achieved through Drouet, but his temporary removal of her deep-seated fears of poverty ironically leaves Carrie free to dwell upon her other desires, and these thoughts cause dissatisfaction. Drouet also has given her money, as much as is essential, and clothes suitable to her position. Yet in riding out with Mrs. Hale north along Lake Michigan toward Evanston and in witnessing the mansions there, seeing private carriages with footmen, the broad lawns, the rich interiors glowing with lamps, Carrie feels her unsatisfied yearnings rise again. "She was perfectly certain that there was happiness. If she could but stroll up yon broad walk, cross that rich entrance-way. . . oh! how quickly would sadness flee." This is Carrie's lot, a plaintive reaching out for the will-o'-the-wisp of lasting happiness and final satisfaction.

Carrie is ripe for change, awaiting only a "magnet," a lightning stroke of chance, to draw her away from Drouet as Drouet had drawn her from her sister's home. Hurstwood assumes this function; and he, a dupe of fate, sacrifices himself in the process.

"The Idea of Hurstwood"

It is not uncommon to speak of *Sister Carrie* as a love story; but although the surface events of the novel appear to parallel those of many a tale of passion, love as it is conventionally understood plays no genuine role in Carrie's life. In her life, other needs, other drives are all-consuming. She feels affection, tenderness even, but only weakly and occasionally; and her heart never rules her head. Whatever elements of love or passion are involved in the novel are furnished by Hurstwood, who finds himself more and more deeply enmeshed in a tangled web.

A man of 40, married to a shrew, father to two indifferent and insufferably snobbish children (the entire family, very like Carrie but more open, is crazy for wealth and status), Hurstwood stands at the apex of his career, solidly established in a fine and lucrative position. He has little to gain and a whole world to lose. Dreiser was interested always in the power of society to create, to mold, or to smash at will. Often in his fictional works the fragility of the human position is treated, but never more pointedly than in his description of Hurstwood's fall. Forgetting the vulnerability of a man of his age, in his exposed position, Hurstwood imagines himself the youth of 20 years past, free to court the object of his passion openly. "A man can't be too careful" had in former days been his usual remark to express a lack of sympathy for compatriots who slipped and were trapped by their mistakes – but now he ignores his own advice.

Blinded by his passion for Carrie, Hurstwood makes his own fatal errors. Unknowingly, he is seen at McVicker's Theater with Carrie and Drouet. He is spied riding in an open carriage with Carrie. Attending an amateur theatrical in which Carrie participates, he rashly explains his wife's absence by insisting she is too ill to attend. Her husband's indiscretions being duly reported to Mrs. Hurstwood, there follow rapidly vehement accusations on her part, an inept handling of the situations on his. Ultimately his wife files a scandalous divorce suit.

The end to Hurstwood's predicament occurs in an action of the most crucial relevance. In its dramatization of man's ultimate helplessness against the forces that prod him, Dreiser's handling of the theft at Hannah and Hogg's easily ranks among the half-dozen most telling scenes in all his work. A perfectly balanced combination of motive and accident leads Hurstwood to commit a crime that will destroy him. Here Dreiser vividly shows the weakness of the human will: in moments of panic a desperate person is likely to grasp at any apparent solution that suggests itself. For the moment, illusion overwhelms reality.

Intensely motivated by the impending notoriety that threatens to cost him his managerial position at the saloon, Hurstwood's judgment falters. He is alone, closing Hannah and Hogg's for the night, dreading the next day when his wife's lawyers have threatened to file suit in court. How will his employers react? Will he lose his family, his property, his position and, because of these, Carrie as well?

The bar's safe has been left unlocked by accident, and Hurstwood glances idly inside. Ten thousand dollars in ready money. He removes the bills, then puts the money back and paces about the room, his brain afire. "Surely no harm could come from looking at it!" He takes the money from the safe again, decides he will abscond with it: "Why, he could live quietly with Carrie for years." He goes so far as to stuff the money into his hand satchel, bills and loose change alike. Then he thinks of scandal, the police, himself a fugitive from justice – ultimately perhaps prison bars. Faced by such prospects, he recoils, self-interest reasserting itself. He lays the money back in the safe, is about to snap the door shut when he realizes the bills and change have been replaced in the wrong boxes. He lifts the boxes out and shifts their contents. While the money is in his hand, the lock clicks. "It had sprung. Did he do it?" A fine ambiguity is established.

Now panic takes over. Hurstwood rushes to Carrie's flat. On the pretext that Drouet has been hurt, he persuades her to board a train with him. The next morning they are in Montreal. But almost at once Hurstwood's employers hire a detective. Within a few days Hurstwood has been intimidated into returning all but $1,300; in exchange, Hannah and Hogg agree not to prosecute. Hurstwood and Carrie board the train for New York, she knowing nothing about the theft.

From this climactic episode, the novel chronicles the steady decline of Hurstwood and the corresponding rise of Carrie. The tone is set at once: "Whatever a man like Hurstwood could be in Chicago, it is very evident that he would be but an inconspicuous drop in an ocean like New York . . . Hurstwood was nothing" (*Carrie*, 321).

Hurstwood retrenches. Instead of battling to rise, he gazes back upon the ruin of his previous career. Obsessed with all he has forfeited, he strives only to safeguard his reduced position against further loss. In this fight, luck turns against him. After he invests the bulk of his capital in a saloon partnership, the building in which he holds his lease is sold to make room for a new edifice.

Stranded without funds, Hurstwood hunts for employment as manager, then as clerk, finally as anything he can obtain. It is a winter of mass unemployment, and his search proves futile. His self-confidence deteriorates. He withdraws farther. His natty appearance by degrees becomes untidy, then slovenly. He and Carrie move from

poor to even tackier quarters. He resorts to gambling. Soon, of the
$700 he possessed when his saloon closed, only a few cents remain.

Meanwhile, convinced she has recklessly immolated herself by
sticking with her lover through his long dark jobless months, Carrie
grows irritable. When it is clear the man's money is all but exhausted,
she puts her clever mind to work, recalls the amateur dramatics that
had afforded her a moderate success in Chicago, makes the rounds
of the theaters, and at last locates an inconspicuous position in a
musical-comedy chorus. Before long, largely through luck, she has
become the breadwinner. Now, in her relationship with Hurstwood,
Carrie senses a trap, and one evening Hurstwood returns from
tramping the streets to find her gone and a brusque note left behind,
one which expresses the heart of Carrie's pragmatic view of life: "I'm
going away. I'm not coming back any more. It's no use trying to keep
up the flat; I can't do it. I wouldn't mind helping you, if I could, but I
can't support us both, and pay the rent. I need what little I make to
pay for my clothes. I'm leaving twenty dollars. It's all I have just now.
You can do whatever you like with the furniture. I don't want it"
(*Carrie*, 484). The denouement of Dreiser's story follows Carrie and
Hurstwood to the logical dead ends of their respective routes. For
Hurstwood there is an accelerated lapse into beggary, a final "What's
the use?" as he opens the gas jets in a 15-cent flophouse, and eventually a plot in potter's field for an unmourned, nameless hulk whom
luck deserted.

As for Carrie, she "found her purse bursting with good green
bills of comfortable denominations. . . . She could look about on her
gowns and carriage, her furniture and bank account" (*Carrie*, 554).
Gone are the days when she had sat in her rocking chair and
dreamed "Ah money, money, money! What a thing to have. How
plenty of it would clear away all these troubles." She has reached the
pot at the end of her rainbow and found it empty; the baubles that
so recently seemed essential are "now grown trivial and indifferent."
Drouet, coming back into the story, is unchanged, still selling, still
prosperous, still chasing women. He is desirous of reestablishing
himself with Carrie. But Carrie dismisses him. She has changed, yet in
exactly what way is unclear. The road ahead is dim. Another man,
Bob Ames, an engineer, has "pointed out a farther step," the possibility for her of a career in straight dramatic roles. Somehow, somewhere, there must be more to life than Carrie has so far tasted, things

to be had beyond "the tinsel and shine of her state" that will bring her to final happiness. She struggles to know what they might be and how she may attain fulfillment.

Rocking to Dreamland

Throughout *Sister Carrie,* Dreiser employs the rocking chair to symbolize the restlessness and the feverish activity that transport Carrie to no satisfying destination. At her sister's flat she had rocked by the window, dreaming of escape with Drouet from the humdrum life of West Van Buren Street. As Drouet's mistress in Ogden Place, she sat in her rocker hungering after luxury, refinement, applause. Living with Hurstwood in New York, she sits rocking to and fro, thinking how "commonplace" her pretty flat is compared with "what the rest of the world [is] enjoying." Carrie always anticipates, discarding and leaving behind her like a locust husk whatever has served its purpose and is no longer of use.

By way of contrast, Hurstwood, after losing his saloon, resorts to the rocking chair merely to brood over days gone by, positions lost, strength waned, funds exhausted. In the chair's steady back and forth motion, he finds an opium dream of security.

Our last view of Carrie is appropriate. Rocking in her chair, successful but unhappy, accomplished but unfulfilled, she dreams of further conquests that will – must – bring her lasting joy; yet she is driven to acknowledge for the first time that happiness may possibly never be for her, that perhaps her fate is "forever to be the pursuit of that radiance of delight which tints the distant hilltops of the world."

Carrie has arrived in her quest at the empty terminal, which, Dreiser points out, so many Americans finally reach, particularly those who clamber up from lowly beginnings and are hoodwinked by the world into believing that money is the ultimate ideal:

> Unfortunately the money problem, once solved, is not the only thing in the world. Their lives, although they reach to the place where they have gold signs, automobiles and considerable private pleasures, are none the more beautiful. Too often, because of these early conditions, they remain warped, oppressive, greedy and distorted in every worthy mental sense by the great fight they have made to get their money. Nearly the only ideal that is set

before these strugglers . . . is the one of getting money. A hundred thousand
children . . . are inoculated in infancy with the doctrine that wealth is all the
shabbiest and most degrading doctrine that can be impressed upon anyone.[2]

Carrie cannot escape her lot. By her adoption of the illusory
values of the social system that she enters when she boards the
Chicago train, she becomes fully as much a victim as Hurstwood of
the great forces that govern human life. Their bankruptcies differ
only in kind, and Carrie's is by far the more ironic.

We leave Carrie where we probably should, on the brink of the
immense and soul-rending discovery that she, no less than George
Hurstwood, has been made the victim of the American system. It
would be a mistake, though an understandable one, for Carrie or her
readers to believe that she has charted her own course; for Dreiser
warns that "the illusion of the self-made is one of the greatest of
all."[3] Carrie is Carrie still, even in prosperity a waif amid forces,
enticed into the quicksands of materialism by those "mirages of
success that hang so alluringly in amethyst skies."

Chapter Three

The Washerwoman's Daughter: *Jennie Gerhardt*

" 'Tis a Sad Story, Mates"

American letters, as the twentieth century dawned, were still mired hand and foot in the tar pits of nineteenth-century gentility. Realists – and naturalists (like Dreiser) in particular – had not yet fully broken away from William Dean Howells's dictum that American writers should expect to stay within the broad average of life, put an emphasis on the sunny side, and publish for public consumption nothing which could not be "openly spoken of before the tenderest society bud at dinner."[1]

Popular writers of the era, such as the Reverend Harold Bell Wright and Gene Stratton Porter (a fellow Hoosier against whose astronomical sales records Dreiser's old Warsaw neighbors assessed his relative literary insignificance), dominated the best-seller lists. In their tales, virtue was its own defense, truth crushed to earth was bound to rise again, and life generally was characterized by swift administration of poetic justice.[2] Stories hinting that the wages of sin might be success or that the transgressor might find a path other than that of thorny retribution were considered to be compatible perhaps with the jaded palates of a decadent European audience whose corrupt appetites glutted on Balzac and Zola, but most Americans wanted it made clear that life this side of the Atlantic thrived on fresher, purer, more wholesome fare.

In this atmosphere *Sister Carrie,* glorifying a heroine who sinned against current mores and prospered, seemed a calculated affront to public morals; it was not to be condoned. The account of the book's suppression, told and retold, varies in its details according to the teller; but Dreiser's own version, surely no less reliable in its outlines

than another, does double service by casting substantial light on the
literary situation then prevailing:

> I took the book to Doubleday, Page & Co. At that time Doubleday had newly
> parted from McClure and had employed Frank Norris as a reader of
> manuscripts. It was Norris who first read the book. He sent for me and he told
> me quite enthusiastically that he thought it was a fine book, and that he was
> satisfied that Doubleday would be glad to publish it. . . . About a week or ten
> days later I had a letter from Walter H. Page, the late ambassador, who asked
> me to call. And when I came he congratulated me on the character of the work
> and announced that it was to be accepted for publication, and that he would
> send me a contract which I was to sign. Also, because he appeared to like the
> work very much, he announced that no pains would be spared to launch the
> book properly, and that – (the glorious American press agent spirit of the
> day, I presume) – he was thinking of giving me a dinner, to which various
> literary people would be invited in order to attract attention to the work and
> to me. . . . Frank Doubleday, the head of the house, was in England at the
> time. In my absence he returned and hearing, as I was afterwards informed,
> that the book was much thought of, decided to read it or, at least, have it read
> for himself. Accordingly . . . he took the book home and gave it to his wife.
> Being of a conventional and victorian turn, I believe – (I have always been
> told so) – she took a violent dislike to the book and proceeded to discourage
> her husband as to its publication. He in turn sent for me and asked me to
> release him from the contract which had already been signed. . . . And
> Doubleday finding that I wished to stand by the contract, announced very
> savagely one day that he would publish the book but that was all he would do.
> I returned to Norris, who said in substance – "Never mind. He'll publish
> it. And when it comes out I'll see that all the worthwhile critics are reached
> with it."
>   . . . When the book came out Norris did exactly as he said. He must have
> written many letters himself for I received many letters commenting on the
> work and the resulting newspaper comment was considerable. However, as
> Mr. Thomas McKee, who was then the legal counsel for Doubleday afterwards
> told me, Doubleday came to him and wanted to know how he could be made
> safe against a law suit in case he suppressed the book – refused to distribute
> or sell any copies. And McKee advised him that he could not be made safe –
> that I had rights under the contract which would be enforced by me if I were
> so minded. Nevertheless, as he told me, Doubleday stored all of the 1,000
> copies printed – minus three hundred distributed by Norris – in the base-
> ment of his Union Square plant, and there they remained . . . until
> 1905. . . . At the time of my last conversation with Frank Doubleday I referred
> to the fact that not only Norris but Mr. Page was heartily for the book, and
> that Mr. Page had told me that not only would he be pleased to publish the
> book but that he had proposed . . . getting up a dinner for me. This seemed to

irritate Doubleday not a little, and walking into the next room where Page was sitting at the time at his desk, and asking me to follow him, he said, "Page, did you say to Mr. Dreiser that you really like this book very much and that you intended to make a stir about it and give him a dinner?" And Mr. Page calmly looked at me in the eye and replied, "I never said anything of the kind."

He was a man of about forty-five years of age, I should have said, at that time. I was just twenty-nine and not a little overawed by editors and publishers in general. In consequence, although I resented this not a little, I merely got up and walked out.[3]

Others have pointed out that Dreiser's admitted resentment may have colored his later recollection of the episode. Surely his correspondence with the publisher reveals that he had been aware for some time that the company might be reluctant to publish the novel – that he had, in fact, suggested to Arthur Henry that the manuscript be submitted elsewhere secretly in case Doubleday, Page and Company chose to back out of the agreement. Page himself had written of dissatisfaction, criticizing the mention of real names and places and the choice of characters, whom he found not the kind of people to "interest the great majority of readers." He advised finally that *Sister Carrie* was "not the best kind of book for a young author to make his first book."

To suggest that Dreiser was disappointed at the publisher's action would be to understate its effect; he was staggered. Although his newspaper days had alerted him to the timidity of the American press, he had hoped to find greater freedom with the novel. Instead, he found censorship just as blatantly operative in the field of fiction. Now began Dreiser's long history of warfare with the censors. The war was to continue, hot and cold, for the rest of his life.

The author of *Sister Carrie* was destitute, intensely moody, broken in spirit. There was no money to live on; and Sara Dreiser, partly because of their financial straits but also because the honeymoon fires no longer flared with any brilliance, returned to Missouri until her husband could establish himself professionally and financially. But Dreiser sank even deeper into despair, existing alone in a tiny tenement room and contemplating suicide before his nervous breakdown was recognized for what it was. After the timely intervention of his brother, Paul, Dreiser spent some months at a "rest camp," then did a stint of physical labor on the railroad – occupational therapy aimed at restoring body and mind.[4]

As soon as he felt able to resume fiction writing, Dreiser began his second novel, eventually to be called *Jennie Gerhardt* and to be the story of another transgressor of society's rules of conduct. Between 1901 and 1903 he made a good, if fitful, beginning on the new book but ultimately was compelled to admit that he could not complete a full manuscript, given his uncertain emotional health and the prevailing codes that governed publication in the United States.

Unless he were allowed to write about life truthfully, Dreiser preferred not to write at all. Instead – at least for the time being – he would edit and market the writing of others. In this way, his own immediate need might be satisfied, while the reading public would continue to be given the dreams it preferred and demanded. What seemed at the time a tenable solution to Dreiser's dilemma was, fortunately for American letters, to prove only briefly feasible.

Having reached his decision, Dreiser encountered no difficulty in establishing himself solidly in the magazine field. In 1904, recovered from his breakdown, he went to work for Street and Smith, publishers of dime novels. The next year he rose to the editorship of the company's new *Smith's Magazine;* in 1906 he moved to the *Broadway Magazine* at a very respectable $65 a week. His remarkable success with these periodicals led to an invitation to supervise the Butterick publications, a combine of three magazines, which at that time constituted a minor publishing empire. The chief magazine, the *Delineator,* was placed under his direct editorship. In a word, he had arrived.

At $7,000 a year, Dreiser's financial worries now seemed a thing of the past. He was well on his way to becoming an influence to be reckoned with in the magazine world. But despite his splendid salary, he was not doing the work he was meant for, and it was only a matter of time until such a patent conflict of interests would become unbearable. Although Dreiser's salary rapidly soared to an unbelievable $10,000 a year, he could not remain contented in the Butterick harness. By 1909 he was moonlighting, editing a magazine of his own, the *Bohemian,* which allowed him more freedom and variety. His personal life also was in turmoil, his marriage falling apart as he became ever more convinced of basic and irremediable incompatibilities between him and his wife. Perhaps he should never have gone through with a marriage in the face of his conviction that monogamy was not for him. As he and Sara drifted into a separation that was to become permanent, Dreiser became involved with the young daughter of an employee at Butterick's. The girl's mother threatened to expose him publicly, creating a ruinous scandal. All signs pointed to the likelihood that he would be dismissed from his editorship. To avoid this, he announced in October 1910 that he was severing his connections with the Butterick organization.

Sister Carrie's Sister

From now on Dreiser intended to work for no man but himself and to devote himself to his writing. His spirits had been restored somewhat by the British success of *Sister Carrie* in 1901 and by the book's American reissue in 1907 by B. W. Dodge and Company to a good deal of critical acclaim. After breaking with his wife and resigning his position with Butterick's, he turned his full attention to completing *Jennie Gerhardt* for publication by Harper & Brothers. Published in 1911, the book was praised by Dreiser's new friend H. L. Mencken as the best American novel ever written, with the single exception of *Huckleberry Finn.*

For *Jennie Gerhardt*, as for aspects of *Sister Carrie*, Dreiser used memories of his sisters' lives for material, but his new book was strikingly different. Carrie's driving self-interest had assured her survival, but hers was far from being the whole story; turned over, the coin revealed another face:

> There is a type of mind or intelligence that seems to leap into the world full-armed and as though equipped by previous experience elsewhere to move without error or faltering here. On the other hand, there is a lesser order of force, equally intuitive and possibly even more sensitive, which, like some of the hardy though none-the-less gorgeous flowers, requires special nurture in order to bring it to its proper stature and value. The hardy weed that fights and in the face of obstacles and oppositions comes to such beauty as is in it, we can admire for its courage as well as forgive its defects. But of the sensitive soul that requires both shelter and aid in order to be all that it might be, and yet fails of the same, what shall we say? (*Dawn*, 147)

If Carrie is a weed equipped to thrust its way sunward against the hostility of its environment, Jennie is the fragile blossom that, deprived of care and protection, will be trampled underfoot. Whereas Carrie is all ambition, Jennie is all love and affection. In his

sisters Dreiser had seen much of Jennie – and even more in his
mother's sweet nature. There he found each of Jennie's virtues:
compassion, gentleness, a yielding softness, generosity, selfless love,
and a fidelity that "would follow love anywhere."

Perhaps because *Jennie Gerhardt* appeared 20 years after the
death of his mother and the dispersion of the family, Dreiser felt
unconstrained about drawing on these early biographical experiences for fiction. Accordingly, where Carrie's novelistic life begins
only after she has parted from her family, Jennie's family circle dominates the first half of her story. *Jennie Gerhardt* is based more
explicitly on the Dreiser family than any other of the author's novels
(though *The "Genius"* is more revelatory of the author's young
manhood), and the destitution Dreiser experienced as a boy is
utilized for full impact. The Gerhardts exist beneath the shadow of
poverty as if under a precipitous cliff of shale that threatens with the
slightest earth tremor to thunder down on them. Every action is
colored by lack of money; life is lived breathlessly in a day-to-day
battle for survival. One by one the Dreiser family members reveal
their identities. There is John Paul Dreiser in the guise of William
Gerhardt, a glassblower out of a job, a fanatic Lutheran with whom
"religion was a consuming thing" and God a tangible personality, "a
dominant reality." There is the mother, gentle, resourceful in
poverty, concerned first, last, and always with her children's welfare,
reduced to scrubbing stairs and taking in washing to keep her family
alive. And there are the children, not so numerous as their real-life
counterparts, to be certain, but quite a house-filling brood nevertheless – six of them, equally divided into boys and girls. Sebastian
(Bass) and Genevieve (Jennie) are the two eldest and the only ones
who play substantial roles in the story.

Bass is a male version of Carrie Meeber. At 19 he has already
"formulated a philosophy of life. To succeed one must do something
– one must associate or at least seem to associate, with those who
were foremost in the world of appearances. . . . Clothes were the
main touchstone. If men wore nice clothes and had rings and pins,
whatever they did seemed appropriate."[5] Like Carrie, then, Bass will
get on in the world. His self-interest will protect him like a coat of
mail as he encounters the "tremendous forces among which we
walk." But Jennie, "poor little earthling, caught in the enormous grip
of chance," wears no such armor.

"When Lovely Woman Stoops to Folly"

When William Gerhardt is ill and out of work, his wife musters her courage and seeks work as a charwoman at the most imposing hotel in Columbus, Ohio. Out of pity, the manager – he really needs no new workers – assigns her to scrubbing the marble stairs. Emboldened by this turn of fortune, the mother pushes her luck one step further. Might she also take in laundry for some of the gentlemen guests of this "palace"? Yes, one guest, a Senator Brander, has washing to be done. This triggers a series of events. Eighteen-year-old Jennie delivers the packet of laundered shirts and linens, and the senator, deeply affected by the girl's beauty and poverty, tips her with a $10 bill. What follows seems natural.

Jennie becomes pregnant. Senator Brander dies unexpectedly of typhoid in Washington before he can fulfill his promise of marriage. The strict Lutheran father, horrified at the breach of his religious code, turns his back on Jennie and drives her from the family home. After Jennie's daughter, Wilhelmina Vesta, is born, William Gerhardt relents somewhat; but he thaws with such glacial slowness that father and daughter are not reconciled until enough years have passed for him to learn that, of all his children, Jennie can least be said to have "gone to the bad."

Bass, in Cleveland working for a cigar store, sends for Jennie, and before long the mother and younger children join them there. The parallel with the actual Chicago adventures of the Dreiser family is strong. The father remains in Ohio, where he has located a position. The exactitude of Dreiser's adherence to biographical fact is felt particularly in his account of the Cleveland domestic arrangement, with its centripetal action around the mother, its pooling of resources for common survival, its infinite concern with the dollars and cents that are its foundation.

Jennie, now an unmarried mother – an extremely risky theme in 1911 – is hired as a maid by the wealthy Bracebridges. Here she meets their house guest, Lester Kane, a bachelor of 36 possessed of immense charm and self-assurance. Feeling "magnetically and chemically drawn" to Jennie, Lester soon declares bluntly, "You belong to me." He trusts his own irresistibility: "He had only to say 'Come' and she must obey; it was her destiny."

As for Jennie, "horrified, stunned, like a bird in the grasp of a cat," she too is at the mercy of life's "chemisms," and of course her grinding poverty helps to dictate the nature of her response. Lester rather easily persuades the girl to accompany him to New York, and the trip is condoned by Mrs. Gerhardt, who sees in Lester's magnanimous gift of $250 "the relief from all her woes – food, clothes, rent, coal – all done up in one small package of green and yellow bills."

For a time, the careers of Jennie and Carrie seem roughly parallel; for each, Cinderella tatters have blossomed into silks. But here the similarity ends. Jennie may be impressed with her bodily adornment, but it is never the clothes themselves she cares about but Lester. Clothes are far from becoming any sort of an end in themselves. Jennie's elemental happiness springs from satisfaction in being dressed suitably for her position as Lester's mistress.

When Jennie and Lester set up housekeeping in North Side Chicago and their "love nest" is discovered by his sister Louise, the Kane family is scandalized. They object not because Lester is indulging in a love affair but because this particular liaison bears dangerous implications of permanence. All the family members are eager for Lester to assume his filial obligations toward the family enterprises. For business reasons, they regard Lester's marriage with a woman of his own class as imperative and do everything in their power to persuade him to break with Jennie. Under tremendous social pressure, Lester earns the reader's sympathy as he persists in his refusal to desert the girl he has seduced and all but married.

The serpent that eventually spoils Jennie's Eden is the familiar force of circumstance: in Brander's case, it had been the accident of death; in Lester's, it is the coercive strength wielded by society and economics. Against such powers, Dreiser demonstrates, love may hold out for a time but eventually stands defenseless.

If Lester appears to be ready to stand by Jennie, come what may, Jennie is prepared to step out of the picture gracefully in order to minimize his forfeitures. In a stormy scene, her renunciation is refused; and Lester moves with her and Vesta to a home in the Hyde Park area of Chicago and brings old Gerhardt, now a widower, to live with them. There Lester learns part of the heavy price society will exact in payment for his transgression. It occurs to him that for some time old friends have avoided his company. When by chance he encounters some of them on the streets, their ambiguous remarks slice like razors. His family hardens against him. Reporters get wind of the story and mercilessly lay it bare in the tabloids, complete with photographs and the headline "THIS MILLIONAIRE FELL IN LOVE WITH THIS LADY'S MAID." The ensuing wreckage of Lester's social hopes is total.

Handfuls of Borrowed Jewels

The death of his father forces Lester to a decision. Archibald Kane has provided in his will that Lester must leave Jennie or marry her; he is to receive a token $10,000 a year for life if marriage is the decision, but he will come into a much larger share of the fortune if he leaves her. Economics is a powerful force; it rules the circles into which Lester was born and now tempts him beyond his endurance. He is 46, and the ardor that once triumphed over all other drives in his nature has cooled somewhat with age. To his family's considerable relief, Lester chooses the practical route. But he does not abandon Jennie without feeling simultaneously "that painful sense of unfairness which comes to one who knows that he is making a sacrifice of virtues – kindness, loyalty, affection – to policy." True to her own affectionate nature, Jennie is eager to make Lester's decision as painless as possible; she is also fully aware that "she had been living in a dream . . . humble, out of place, holding handfuls of jewels that did not belong to her." To relinquish, to renounce – this she had always been prepared to do. Now in her magnanimity she is willing to hand Lester over to the society woman who claims to have loved him since girlhood.

The surface life, appearances, what people think – these things do not hold much interest for Jennie. "Affection was what she craved. Without it she was like a rudderless boat on an endless sea." So long as she remains positive of Lester's affection, Jennie is satisfied to free him and allow appearances to take what shape they may. Her stoicism comes to the fore: "They would be dead after a little while, she and Lester and all these people. Did anything matter except goodness – goodness of heart? What else was there that was real?"

In drawing such a portrait and basing an entire novel on it, Dreiser ran a considerable risk. The self-sacrificing heroine was a staple of the popular sentimental novels that he disdained. The too-good-to-be-true wife went back to the story of patient Griselda that Chaucer told in the fifteenth century, and it was far from being new even then. But, difficult as it is to accept such a portrait in modern times, Dreiser succeeds to a remarkable degree in depicting Jennie's soft yielding without making her laughably unreal. Somehow, the personality of Jennie manages to rise above mere sentimentality and to take shape as a recognizable human figure. What might all too easily have been soggy and maudlin becomes poignant, and through painstaking characterization, Dreiser's Jennie eventually far outruns his Carrie in achieving a philosophical position where genuine happiness is not only possible but lies reasonably within human grasp. As for Lester, in his weakness he reiterates the familiar Dreiser position on the world at large, explaining lamely to the woman he is in fact deserting: "All of us are more or less pawns. We're moved about like chessmen by circumstances over which we have no control."

Jennie's vindication arrives when Lester, now nearing 60, calls her to his side in his final illness. Dying, he desires only her; and, despite all his neglect, this last unmistakable token of his affection compensates Jennie for her sacrifice. In her own way, she is happy, even though the people of Lester's world will have none of her. As she stands in the dark shadows at the railroad station watching Lester's coffin being loaded, she ponders: "Was not life a patchwork of conditions made and affected by these things which she saw – wealth and force – which had found her unfit? She had evidently been born to yield, not seek. This panoply of power had been paraded before her since childhood. What could she do now but stare vaguely after it as it marched triumphantly by? Lester had been of it. Him it respected. Of her it knew nothing" (*Jennie*, 430).

The novel's ending, though it does leave Jennie suspended between present and future, is replete with implications of happiness – or at least of peace and contentment – that render it a far more optimistic work than *Sister Carrie*. It is quite obvious to the reader that Dreiser is himself deeply emotionally involved with his creation. Dreiser does not ever display much affection for Carrie, although he does seem to admire her grit and persistence in making her way upward. She is Dreiser's "little pilgrim" who does what she feels she must do to prosper in her headlong pursuit of riches and fame, but he never appears to feel for her even a spark of the tenderness that infuses every paragraph of Jennie's tale. Dreiser's "pet heroine"[6] is left not destitute but occupied with the rearing of two orphan children she has adopted (her own Vesta has died of typhoid some years before – another borderline lapse into sentimentality).

"And then what?" asks the author. The question is pertinent, for while Carrie's inevitable frustration was quite explicitly forecast, Jennie's future is left open for the reader to surmise. Such an ambiguity stands by itself as a sizable concession for a master naturalist to make. Dreiser's dilemma seems clear. On the one hand, he sees Jennie as being eminently worthy of the best that life can bestow; on the other, he is committed to his stark view of life in which the worthy, justly or unjustly, are thwarted by circumstance.

And then what, indeed? Jennie will not be immune to loneliness, to disappointment, or to further rejection by society. Yet she cannot help but prosper in her own way. "We live in an age in which the impact of materialized forces is well-nigh irresistible; the spiritual nature is overwhelmed by the shock," announced Jennie's author in explaining Lester Kane's position on life. It is to Jennie's everlasting credit and well-being that she manages consistently to resist the impact of these forces. She invariably asks the right questions. Carrie had inquired only: "What is there to be had? How can I best get it, and quickly?" Jennie asks: "Why? Why has all this happened, and why am I the way I am and others the way they are?" Carrie is oriented to the exterior life; Jennie, to the interior. And this will be her salvation.

"Did anything matter except goodness – goodness of heart? What else was there that was real?" By posing the question rather than answering it, Dreiser reveals his own deep skepticism; for the method by which his world has organized itself leaves scant room for natural affections and holds goodness of heart very cheap indeed. In a society where only caste and class matter, passivity dooms one to fruitless waiting outside doors that will never yield. It seems clear that in *Jennie Gerhardt* Dreiser is paying a tribute to the pliable and affectionate personality of his mother. To achieve it required that he avert his gaze for a moment from some of the most bitter truths he had to tell about life. In the body of his work there is no other story like *Jennie Gerhardt*, and in his later novels Dreiser hewed a good deal closer to the stark vision of the true literary naturalist.

Chapter Four

Financier, Titan, and Stoic:
A Trilogy of Desire

"The Discovery That Even Giants Are But Pygmies"

"A hell of a fine novel is going to be written about some of these things one of these days," remarked John Maxwell of the *Globe* to Theodore Dreiser (*Myself*, 68). The two men – editor and cub reporter – were speculating on the drama of the current scene in their Chicago. On a daily basis they observed machinations little different from those prevailing in other burgeoning American industrial centers where "cat-like" dynasty builders and financiers, "the coldest, the most selfish, and the most useful"[1] of beings, maneuvered to erect their thrones of power.

In Dreiser's city one man in particular was dominating these early 1890s: Charles T. Yerkes. A financial wizard who recognized no laws but his own, this entrepreneurial Goliath bestrode the "narrow Chicago world like a colossus," tooling his way into supremacy over the city's streetcar networks, buying city councils and mayors as he might purchase bonbons at a confectionery counter, and generally remolding the financial life of the young midwestern metropolis to promote his own grandiose schemes.

Twenty years later, after Yerkes had abandoned Chicago for richer bonanzas in England, only to be stricken down a hairbreadth short of total victory, and after Dreiser also had deserted Chicago for New York City and achievement as a novelist, life was breathed into editor Maxwell's idle remark by the publication of "a hell of a fine novel" indeed. It was *The Financier*, based closely on Yerkes's life and ultimately to be the first volume of Dreiser's auspicious *A Trilogy of Desire*. Hard upon its heels appeared the second volume, *The Titan*. But it would take another 30 years for the concluding book, *The Stoic*, to reach the public.

47

This triple-decker, which critic Ellen Moers calls "the most valuable historical fiction produced in this country,"[2] begins with the
Philadelphia boyhood and rise to power of a born financier. Frank
Algernon Cowperwood is rapacious by nature, a classic Machiavellian. Even as a young boy he knows how to cut a deal to his own
profit, and before he turns 30 he is rich. Temporarily checkmated in
his native Philadelphia and hungry for new worlds to conquer,
Cowperwood invades Chicago. There he consolidates the street rail-
ways into a monopoly and approaches a state of absolute power
before that city's populace rises to stop him. Then he adroitly shifts
to England with a program for snaring control of the London subway
system. With death striking him down ironically on the eve of his
conquest, Cowperwood's properties, mortgaged to the hilt, fall into
the hands of receivers to be devoured by "legal vultures." Cotermi-
nous with this extended chronicle of big business is the running
account of Cowperwood's amatory adventures – two unhappy
marriages and the most amazing chorus line of mistresses seen in
American literature up to that time. Dreiser's inclusion of this parade
of beauties prompted critic Stuart P. Sherman to lambaste the trilogy
as a "huge club sandwich composed of slices of business alternating
with erotic episodes."[3] The comment is somewhat on target because,
as a work of art, A Trilogy of Desire is flawed; too much of everything
is included, and the author's preoccupation with infinite details of
business and sex may finally explain the lack of total satisfaction
experienced by his many sympathetic readers and friendly critics.

"Giants Fighting, Plotting, Dreaming"

With the Trilogy, Dreiser leaves "fallen women" like Carrie Meeber
and Jennie Gerhardt to focus on the American financial tycoon of the
late nineteenth century. Although Dreiser was anything but a slavish
follower of fashion, the subject of the Trilogy capitalized on a main
current of topical interest. Since the Civil War, average Americans
had watched, half dazed, half entranced, while finance and enterprise flourished on an unprecedented scale. For the first time, industrial-era corporations and utility combines were shaped in the
modern pattern, marked by common characteristics: massiveness,
concentrated wealth, octopuslike tenacity and reach, untold power

seized through piratical methods or legislative corruption, and a fundamental contempt for public opinion.

As the implications of this unbridled power struggle in "the land of the free" slowly dawned upon the citizenry, and particularly upon the writers, "the shadow of the muckrake" fell over the land. It became permissible for "captains of industry" to be unmasked as "robber barons." Condemnations of big-business monopoly cropped up in the press; magazines and newspapers found exposés so profitable that few areas of public life were left undisturbed. One by one, the largest areas of industrial-era problems – the oil monopoly, slums, factory conditions, child labor, insurance, wheat and beef production, railroads, city government – were subjected to microscopic examination. *McClure's Magazine,* to which Dreiser himself contributed shortly after the turn of the century, marshalled such angry writers as Roy Stannard Baker *(The Subway Deal),* Lincoln Steffens *(Chicago: Half Free and Fighting On),* Burton J. Hendrick *(The Making of Great Fortunes),* and Ida Tarbell *(History of the Standard Oil Company).* A favorite of Dreiser's was Gustavus Myers's three-volume *History of the Great American Fortunes,* which accomplished in nonfiction something akin to what Dreiser was attempting in fiction. Imaginative writers Frank Norris and Jack London and others joined their voices with the chorus of professional muckrakers who were deploring the evils rampant in the mushrooming growth of industrialism, and Upton Sinclair in *The Jungle* (1906) devoted a novel to the story of labor problems and food contamination in the great Union Stockyards of Chicago.

It was little wonder then that Dreiser, who had seen the corruption of his times up close, should write in a similar vein. Muckraking aside, however, Dreiser's chief concern was with the individual's relationship to society. He both respected and feared the omnipotence of society, but he did not believe – as *Sister Carrie* and *Jennie Gerhardt* might have seemed to imply – that nature intended the force of society always to win. Dreiser dreamed of powerful, magnetic, dominant individuals untrammeled by codes or caste. In some ways they seemed to represent an ideal, even a pernicious one. Dreiser himself was far from being such a man, and most of his fellows citizens, he was fairly certain, were even more intimidated and inhibited than himself.

Dreiser was fond of conjuring up the image of men with strength enough to rise boldly to their full stature and tell society to go to hell, to choose their own battlefields on which they might challenge society's massive power – and win. Writing the *Trilogy* allowed Dreiser to argue that the individual need not succumb invariably to society. But before such a story could take shape, he needed a central figure to play superman: someone who would not, could not, knuckle under. Where, in America, was such a man? The only place he saw a model available was in the economic marketplace.

"The Pathology of the Genus Financier"

It saddened Dreiser that only in the field of finance could America exhibit to the world a group of exceptional individuals who might be compared favorably with the superachieving heroes of other lands. Why this should be so, Dreiser did not understand; and he deplored the fact that his country did not shine as brightly in the arts, in philosophy, or even in politics as it did in commercial enterprise.

What was this rare breed of men called financiers? How were they set apart from mortal men? To begin with, they seemed to be born for the roles they played. One could no more become a financier by wishing it than he could add an inch to his natural height. To Dreiser the genius for organizing an enterprise seemed to be a gift, just as a great voice, a beauty, or talent for painting are gifts. Once "selected" by nature, the financier was known for his single-minded intensity – "shark-like" is Dreiser's image for it. A financier might be destructive in his avidity, yet nature finally used him as it might use any other implement – and often in ways too devious to be discerned by ordinary people – as a great constructive force in opening the resources of uninhabited areas, laying railroads, building cities and utility systems. In the long haul, a man of apparent evil could produce positive good. It was clear that the financier had no use for such a "frivolous" concept as democracy; the Constitution, the Bill of Rights, or any other set of laws existed merely to invite violation by the strong and bold. But paradoxically, by producing and disseminating goods to the masses, the financier might well serve ultimately as a useful implement for achieving economic democracy.

For the great financier, as Dreiser saw him, sex was less a matter of morality than a question of convenience and animal desire. Often it meant the acquisition of a lovely status symbol, a queen to preside over the social areas of his kingdom. Where his own interests were concerned, any trick or snare was justified. Pettiness was no deterrent to the financier so long as it played its part in achieving success for whatever project his enthusiasm had seized upon. At the same time, he could be capable of immense and seemingly contradictory benefactions; as one might expect, these were designed always to promote his own popularity and thus consolidate his power. The perpetuation of his own fame was his continuing concern.

How then were these titans of the industrial world to be prevented from complete domination of the world? In reading Herbert Spencer's *First Principles*, Dreiser had learned that nature in its inscrutable plan for the world had provided a set of checks and balances that ensured the stability of the total system. By means of what Spencer called "the equation inevitable," willful individuals are born to promote change and reorganize life into new patterns; but at the same time there are born other individuals with opposite tendencies and with the will and the power to resist. Between these two forces an equilibrium, a healthy balance, is maintained. It was quite possible, then, for a man to "be a Colossus and bestride the world without upsetting the equation ultimately."[4]

Nature's way, for Dreiser, was invariably the right way. But the welter of human activity was disorienting. How was one to perceive always and precisely what nature's way might be? There was a clue in Spencer. Since in nature's plan the mass was all, the individual nothing, it was clear that the world would suffer no permanent harm from allowing a financier his deranging but temporary power over conditions (*Hey*, 167-80). All things would pass; the equilibrium would be restored.

As a specimen of *genus Financierus Americanus*, Frank Cowperwood is created free of any of the hobbling limitations that Dreiser usually placed upon his fictional heroes. He is heavily armored for the fray: vital, crafty, completely amoral, driven by desire without limit, supremely confident of his own destiny. Cowperwood runs no risk of the disillusionment that plagued Carrie, because his soul is "as bereft of illusion as a windless moon." For him the illusion *is* reality. Untold sucking in of wealth, ever greater power – these for him are life itself. Set against the power of the true financier, ordinary individuals are as trifling as gnats. If outnumbered, the financier withdraws to strike elsewhere, aware that discretion is the better part of valor. When he slips – which is seldom – he learns from his mistakes how to win in another place, at another time, recouping every loss and advancing. Over such a man, one force alone wields decisive power – nature itself.

The time was ripe for treatment of the financier phenomenon in fiction, but Dreiser was driven also by his own insatiable curiosity about those few favored ones upon whom nature seemed to have lavished all the gifts she had withheld from himself. By inverting his own personality, Dreiser could manage to conjure up a Cowperwood as unlike himself as possible – a dream figure, an ideal. He sets the tone early in the first volume of the *Trilogy:*

> The appearance of young Cowperwood at this time [was] prepossessing and satisfactory. His hair was rather a neutral shade, dark brown. . . . His head was large, shapely . . . and fixed on a square pair of shoulders and a stocky body. Nature had destined him to be five feet ten inches tall. . . . He walked with a light, confident, springy step. Life had given him no severe shocks nor rude awakenings. He had not been compelled to complain of illness or pain or deprivation of any kind. His family was respected; his father well placed. . . . His handsome body, slowly broadening, was nearly full grown. His face, because of its full, clear, big, inscrutable eyes, had an expression which was almost babyish. . . . He looked like a young warrior . . . with his even teeth, his square jaw.[5]

One might contrast this paragon with the self-portrait of the author: a skinny, bean-pole figure and a face with receding chin, splayed teeth, and cast eye. Compare this life with the author's own youth – its poverty, defeated father, and chronic hypochondria. Clearly, Cowperwood is the man Dreiser would love to have been.

Where Dreiser all too often felt himself swept along by the tides of chance, Cowperwood resists these tides, grapples with them, and turns them to his own benefit. Where young Dreiser trembled at the prospect of testing himself with women, Cowperwood, "no trembling novice quailing at every thought of the moral law," has the utmost confidence in his personal magnetism and takes a prodigious series of mistresses, far exceeding even the number hinted at in factual accounts of Yerkes's admittedly sybaritic life.

Dreiser's family moved frequently, always to more destitute quarters; Cowperwood's family moves frequently but always to a richer

neighborhood, a more palatial home. In contrast to Dreiser's financial ineptitude, Cowperwood "from the very first" knows which path
leads to the lode. Strongly possessed by somewhat the same basic
motivations toward money, power, and sex with which he endowed
his financier, Dreiser blamed the arbitrary injustice of nature for not
equipping him with the means of satisfying his desires: "How often
have I looked through the windows of some successful business firm
and wished I had achieved ownership or stewardship, a position
similar to that of any of the officers and managers inside! To be
president or vice-president of something, some great thrashing business of some kind. Great God, how sublime it seemed" (*Myself,* 108).
Only on a cloud of fantasy, in fiction, could Dreiser ride with
Cowperwood the money king into dream worlds of finance and love.

Mr. Yerkes-Cowperwood

Why Dreiser selected Yerkes as his model instead of one of the
better-known financiers whose meteoric careers fascinated him is
not really very difficult to ascertain. Frick, Vanderbilt, Gould, Rockefeller, Astor, Carnegie – any of these might possibly have served as
model. But circumstance had familiarized Dreiser with Yerkes'
manipulations, had seemed in fact to have thrown the two men
together as if for a purpose, first in Chicago and then in New York.
While Dreiser the reporter was struggling to locate his place in the
Manhattan sun, Yerkes the financial genius was ensconced in the
Fifth Avenue mansion from which he worked back and forth across
the Atlantic on his London underground deal. When Yerkes died in
December 1905, the press in all its forms lavished front-page space
on accounts of the funeral, speculation on bequests, and the actual
reading and interpretation of the will. For another five years feature
articles listed the legacies this multimillionaire left behind him and
detailed the fierce legal battles contesting the estate. Edwin Lefevre's
"What Availeth It?"[6] and Charles Russell's "Where Did You Get It,
Gentlemen?"[7] in *Everybody's Magazine* and other muckraking articles kept the story breathing. In 1910 the headlines read "YERKES ART
TREASURES UNDER THE HAMMER"; the marble palace on Fifth Avenue
and all its fabled hoard went to the highest bidder. Soon after, Mrs.
Yerkes died, and the year had scarcely passed before Dreiser, having

mulled over the project for a long while, as was his habit, set to work on the *Trilogy.*

Whether men like Yerkes lived or died, the world would remain the same, according to Herbert Spencer. What useful things Yerkes had bludgeoned into existence would live after him. The people of the cities would ride his transportation networks without a thought for the builder. The rest of his acquisitions, the treasure trove he had guarded more carefully than any dragon, would be dispersed to the four winds. The mansion itself would be dismantled. And Dreiser, having built a superman in his own image, but inverted, could handily destroy the fantasy he had created, bring the dream empire tumbling back to earth again to demonstrate the principle he never relinquished: that nature cares naught for the trees, only for the forest.

To make this eventual summary statement is the function assigned *The Stoic.* In his entire *Trilogy,* Dreiser has two theses to prove. The first is that nature creates these supermen who will dominate and reshape the world against any societal resistance. This point is argued in *The Financier* and brought to fruition in *The Titan.* The second is that nature, having used its human implement to accomplish whatever purpose he was created for, discards him on the rubbish heap. To argue this point is the task of *The Stoic.* Nature retains control. Man remains a creature of illusion.

The boy Cowperwood is furnished early with the proper ethic. At age 10, when passing a fish market near his home, Frank spies a tank in which a lobster has been paired off with a squid. It is a classic image of predator and prey, the law of the jungle displayed in a tub of water. The lobster, heavily weaponed, aggressive, considers the squid his natural victim. The squid is unarmored and lacks any defensive equipment aside from speedy movement (not very useful in a small aquarium) and a soon depleted "smokescreen" of ink. He is doomed. It is only a matter of time before the battle goes to the swift and aggressive lobster. Young Frank Cowperwood ponders this object lesson; it answers for him the riddle of the way life is organized. If lobsters lived on squids, and men lived on lobsters, then what lived on men? A little observing, a little thinking, and the answer arrives: "That was it! Sure, men lived on men."

Once Frank has absorbed this lesson, accepted its principle, and made up his mind to be one of the strong, he has, perhaps without fully willing or realizing it, sloughed off whatever might weaken his chances in the struggle before him – sentiment, Christian morality, concern for anyone except himself.

A Lion in the Streets

Before he is out of his teens, Cowperwood knows all the desires that are to ride him until death looses their hold: desires for success, for women, for beauty, for art, for acceptance and prestige, for immortality. The route to gratification in each area is firmly substructured by his intuitive Machiavellianism. Success in piling up money comes foremost; it stands head and shoulders above any secondary aim. To Cowperwood, "Money was the first thing to have – a lot of it. . . . Then you secured the reputation. The two things were like legs on which you walked."[8]

In the money game, conventional morality or ethics played no part, not because the rules were to be broken but because the world of the financier was a universe apart. The Golden Rule and the thou-shalt-nots of the Ten Commandments could not possibly apply here. Yet, because the financiers were compelled to mingle with their more commonplace terrestrial cousins, the illusion of conformity had to be maintained. It would be useful in hoodwinking society.

The ambiguity through which a man becomes simultaneously a buccaneer and a philanthropist has ever fascinated and perplexed observers of American financial history, notwithstanding the fact that the phenomenon is as old as man himself. Cowperwood intuitively understands that "the thing for him to do was to get rich and hold his own – to build up a seeming of virtue and dignity which would pass muster for the genuine thing" (*Financier*, 244)

As he slashes his path through life, cutting down his opponents with no more mercy or remorse than a reaper feels for the individual stalks of grain, Cowperwood always takes pains to preserve this semblance of conformity in his personal and business affairs. One way to create the mirage is well known and often practiced: public benefaction. Cowperwood's first such gift, the donation of an observatory to the University of Chicago, is motivated by a need to enhance his reputation with other financiers and thus to facilitate the loans he is seeking in New York and in London: "On such repute (the ability to give a three-hundred-thousand-dollar telescope out of hand to be known as the Cowperwood telescope) he could undoubtedly raise money. . . . The whole world would know him in a day. . . . The gift was sufficient to set Cowperwood forth in the light of a public benefactor and patron of science" (*Titan*, 372).

At strategic points in his career, Cowperwood makes certain that people learn of his plan for eventually donating his mansion and his art collection to the city of New York as a monument to his memory, and he reveals the stipulation in his will that provides for the building of a gigantic free Cowperwood Hospital. Both proposals, of course, evaporate after his death; but by then they have already served their purpose.

Secondary to the acquisition of wealth is a mounting desire in Cowperwood for the possession of art – painting, sculpture, tapestries, and rare carpets. The obsession with art is a recurrent oddity of the money king's psychology. It comes as no surprise to discover that this acquisition of art, like public benefaction, is ambiguous at bottom and tainted with the Midas touch. Cowperwood is first inspired by what he feels is an authentic interest in art for art's sake. Then his dealer suggests that great pictures invariably increase in value; an investment of a few hundred thousand cannot help but result in a profit of millions. His financial acumen tells him that the dealer is correct. Accordingly, with one beady eye on the cash register and another on aesthetics, Cowperwood crams his lavish mansion with the conspicuous loot of his travels until it is more a museum than a home. Little would be required but the stationing of an attendant at the front door to convert it at once into a public gallery – which is, in fact, intended to be its ultimate function in Cowperwood's master plan.

Thus Cowperwood embodies every essential trait of the financial titans who, like brontosauruses, stalked through the ooze of the first industrial age and dominated the final quarter of the nineteenth century. Success being an end in and for itself, winning was everything and the only thing. Great wealth (token and proof of victory) was to be gained through Machiavellian practices, if need be, and preserved through force and chicanery. The great financier was to awaken to the desire for beauty and art; and his life, if perfectly realized, was to be rounded by the dream of self-created immortality through philanthropic bequests that would make him a hero in the eyes of his deluded fellow citizens.

Cowperwood's efforts to have his cake and eat it too require a partner. What is a host without a hostess, adorned from head to foot in the best money can buy, to receive his summoned guests? In *The Financier*, Lillian Semple, the first Mrs. Cowperwood, is not up to this task. She is too pale a figure, too retiring, and Cowperwood, the ultimate pragmatist, discards her. In *The Titan*, Cowperwood's social program is put in the hands of his second wife, Aileen Butler Cowperwood. Aside from the titanic figure of her husband who dominates all but the final pages of the *Trilogy*, hers is the most completely realized portrait in the three volumes. Since Aileen's original model is found only sketchily in Dreiser's sources, she is more the product of the artist's creative power than is Cowperwood; and she is fully drawn and altogether believable. The rash, headstrong daughter of a Philadelphia politician, young, gay, colorful, exuberant, she finds herself drawn magnetically to Cowperwood. Her own desires for material success tally with his.

In Philadelphia, the fact that Cowperwood has committed a crime by tampering with civic funds (with the connivance of the City Treasurer) is revealed during the financial panic that follows the great Chicago fire of 1871. Convicted, he is sentenced to a prison term. After his release from the Eastern Penitentiary, Cowperwood marries Aileen. They set out for Chicago to start life afresh, blazing with financial stratagems and plans to penetrate to the heart of a "brilliant society that shone in a mirage." Following an initial flourish of entertainments at which the Cowperwoods mistakenly interpret attendance as acceptance, society barricades its doors. One financier describes Aileen as "charming, but she's hardly cold enough, I'm afraid; hardly clever enough. It takes a more serious type. She's a little too high-spirited. These old women would never want to get near her; she makes them look old. She'd do better if she were not so young and pretty" (*Titan*, 71). Aileen's most appealing traits are thus turned into spears against her. Hints of her previous irregular relationship with Cowperwood are being whispered around the city, and she finds fewer and fewer callers attending her "at homes." So long as she feels that she has her husband's love and support, Aileen can endure the debacle of her social life, but it is not long before she must face the fact that she no longer possesses him solely. His wandering eye has strayed to delights in neighboring pastures. As he flits from woman to woman, she is left at home alone without company, aside from a small army of servants.

In an effort to arouse Cowperwood's jealousy and so win him back, Aileen turns to other men – only to find that her husband is happy to have her so occupied. It leaves him free to dally as he pleases. The bitterness of Aileen's Chicago failure is repeated when the Cowperwoods erect their auspicious citadel on New York's Fifth Avenue. At the time of Frank's death the two of them are estranged. Aileen's sense of outrage vents itself in a last obstinate refusal even to allow his body to be brought into the mansion. Only by bribing the servants could the financier's hirelings manage to bring his coffin inside, and this under cover of night, so that the corpse might lie in state, perpetuating the public facade of domestic harmony.

"A Huge Club Sandwich"

The alienation of Frank and Aileen Cowperwood results from the final controlling desire in the financier's life. Next to self-interest, which to Dreiser always ruled supreme, sex was the most tremendous of forces goading the human creature. In this arena, Frank Cowperwood is as precocious as he is at coining money. At 13 he wins his first girl, the 12-year-old daughter of Quaker neighbors, with the gift of a licorice stick. Although the result is no more momentous than a surreptitious kiss or two stolen at parties or in darkened hallways, Frank rapidly moves on to other girls, to Dora Fitler and to Marjorie Stafford. At this point Dreiser waxes coy: "Shall the story of Marjorie be told? It isn't as innocent as the others. But no, let it go. There will be more than sufficient without it" (*Financier*, 39).

Superhuman in financial dealings, Cowperwood is as vulnerable as ordinary men when it comes to love. Enamored at 19 of one Mrs. Semple, five years his senior and recently widowed, Cowperwood marries without the least perception that his wife and he are temperamentally incompatible. So long as he acts with his brain, Cowperwood is as invincible as human flesh can be. Unfortunately perhaps, men are prone to choose women not intellectually but on an emotional, passionate basis. Cowperwood finds that Lillian Semple's clear skin and fragile beauty charm him like a portrait by the romantic painter Burne-Jones. Desiring her, craving her, he therefore must have her. But he soon tires of Lillian, who ages quickly and, losing her beauty, loses her hold on him as well. Cowperwood turns to Aileen Butler, thus exhibiting an amatory ineptness that is to dog him all his days. For Aileen is the daughter of a financial colleague upon whose good will Cowperwood depends. When Edward Butler is apprised of his daughter's seduction, he relishes taking a hand in exposing Cowperwood and in putting him in Eastern Penitentiary.

Frank Cowperwood's Chicago mistresses parade one by one through the pages of *The Titan* in neatly arranged sequences that create the "club sandwich" effect that peeved critic Stuart Sherman.[9] Once only, when he seduces his secretary, does Cowperwood show any degree of common sense in his choice. His usual mistresses are summoned from among the wives and daughters of associates, men who often stand in a position to do Cowperwood genuine harm.

Only the last of Cowperwood's lovers, the final jewel of his harem, becomes much more than a mere name. Berenice Fleming, daughter of a Louisville brothel madam, is barely 16 when her blonde beauty catches Cowperwood's eye. Then he decides that of all the women in the world – and he has known his share of them – this is the one he wants, the one he must possess, the one destined for him. Stepping out of character a bit to do so, perhaps, Cowperwood determines not to seduce Berenice; instead he waits stoically for her to come to him or not, as she will. She resists Cowperwood until word of her mother's past has leaked out, ruining her chances of marrying into society. Berenice then becomes Cowperwood's mistress, as he had hoped and predicted. But it is money, not love, that is the lure. And while she is faithful to the financier, she schemes at the same time to set herself up securely; as she herself puts it, she prefers unhappiness in wealth over happiness in poverty. Berenice figures prominently through half of the *Trilogy*, and she is the only major character active in the last third of *The Stoic*.

"The Glitter Tarnishes"

The assumption of many readers that the *Trilogy* was intended as a celebration of Nietzsche's superman was understandable after the publication of *The Financier* and remained valid after *The Titan* appeared, even though the *Macbeth* allusions ending those novels implied disasters to come (*Financier*, 780; *Titan*, 552). The elements of that superman are undeniably present: the power, the craft, and the anarchy, which raise Cowperwood so far above ordinary men that only titanic and inevitable forces can crush him – huge events such as the Chicago fire, the rising of a citizenry en masse, even the cold hand of death itself. But had Dreiser been bent only on celebrating the financial titan, he would have modeled his financier upon one whose life had ended more happily, whose plans remained unblasted, and whose fortune endured.

Always in his observations of American wealth and power, Dreiser mentioned the contrasting poverty and helplessness that were their corollaries. He was angry that life did not better organize itself so that even though the big brain must dominate the little one, there might be "just a slightly less heavily loaded table for Dives and a few more crumbs for Lazarus." Efforts toward this socially desirable equilibrium are made by Dreiser's insistence in his fiction that even the superman shall be the ultimate pawn of circumstance. And so Dreiser allows the winds of chance to blow through the *Trilogy*, rendering even great men insignificant against powerful forces. The Chicago fire smashes Cowperwood's dreams of conquest in Philadelphia; the failure of the financial house of Jay Cooke re-establishes him as a power. His own death, coming at the worst possible time, demolishes his empire and scatters its ashes.

Furthermore, the Cowperwoods do not escape personal disillusionment. Frank's first marriage ends badly. His second, to Aileen, although built upon grandiose hopes and rosy promises, also breaks on the rocks of circumstance. Their aspirations to social prestige burst like soap bubbles. Only Cowperwood's money remains and, through it, his economic power. Aileen is more cruelly dealt with than her husband. Having staked all on her marriage, she loses all. Dreams of social conquest fade quickly; her husband abandons her for other women; her luxurious home loses whatever meaning it might have had: "The sum and substance of all those years and efforts was that she lived alone, was visited by no true friend, legally defeated in one honest claim after another, until she at last fully realized that the dream of grandeur which this house represented had vanished into thin air."[10] Aileen's final disillusionment arrives as her chauffeur drives her past the forced auction at her Fifth Avenue palace; collectors are bearing away her treasures.

What remains? Edwin Lefevre suggested an answer to the puzzle a full year before *The Financier* appeared in print. Noting the savagery with which Yerkes's estate was looted in death, as the money baron had himself looted in life, he concluded: "The Great American Novel can be nothing but pages taken from the lives of Americans Who Do Things. Only in death is the moral of their tale plain. You read 'Finis' and then you begin to think. The glitter tarnishes; the jingle of the dollar ceases; envy is stilled. What remains. . . . nothing!" (Lefevre, 845).

Berenice

Lefevre was not entirely correct. A good deal remains, more in the novel than in the life. And what does remain explains to some degree why *The Stoic* has been generally recognized as the weakest section of the *Trilogy*. Ideally, a trilogy should be so constructed that a dramatic "build" is maintained, rising to a culmination in the third volume. Instead, the first of Dreiser's three books remains the most absorbing. It is intriguing to watch the youthful Cowperwood grow and expand, attempt and fail, learn and succeed, until he lands on top of the heap. Once there, his fight to remain king of the hill, told in *The Titan*, lacks the involvement of the early struggles. The reader is in danger of being jaded by repetitious acts. *The Stoic*, with its ironic smashing of Cowperwood's dreams, contains potentially the greatest material, surely much more vital than that of *The Titan*, but the novel as written represents a definite falling off. It lacks the zest of the other volumes.

Some blame for the failure of *The Stoic* must be laid on the circumstances surrounding its completion. Finished in Dreiser's last days when, exhausted, he made a final attempt to get the story between covers, the volume was never really completed in the ordinary sense. Everything that matters was at least sketched in, but often the scenes were no more than that: sketches. With Dreiser's health failing, no time remained for revision and final polish. The closing chapters, left in summary, had to be put together by others. Four days before his death, Dreiser wrote to James T. Farrell, his friend and self-chosen critic: "I simply stopped writing at the end because I was tired" (Elias 1959, 3:1035).

What remains in *The Stoic* after Cowperwood's demise is Berenice; and Dreiser makes a mistake in shifting the emphasis to her. This may well be the result of his social consciousness, which had intensified considerably in the years since he first undertook the story of Cowperwood. Perhaps he was convinced the *Trilogy* as it stood did not hammer home its social message forcefully enough. In any case, left now with only Berenice to act upon a stage emptied of other principals, Dreiser invokes a lightning bolt of conscience that strikes Berenice with force sufficient to bring about "the dawn of a spiritual awakening." The girl is transformed from an empty-headed, self-centered odalisque into a yoga-practicing social worker bent on improving slum conditions in New York's Harlem.

She becomes the worst kind of unknowledgeable do-gooder. After a period of years spent in India and experiences that convert her to mysticism, she places her Park Avenue home (a gift from Cowperwood) on the market to raise money. With this sum, augmented by whatever she can finagle out of influential friends, Berenice intends to build the Cowperwood Hospital her lover had dreamed would stand as his monument. In the end she becomes little more than Dreiser's spokesperson, mouthing words that he wanted the *Trilogy* to say. Not having said them elsewhere, he found her a convenient megaphone: "Her entire life, as she realized – with the exception of the past few years – had been spent in the pursuit of pleasure and self-advancement. But now she knew that one must live for something outside of one's self, something that would tend to answer the needs of the many as opposed to the vanities and comforts of the few, of which she herself was one. What could she do to help?" (*Stoic*, 306). "Very little" is the only answer possible, given the magnitude of poverty in America and the world.

The *Trilogy* is not without its faults and its excesses, but it possess great merits as well as defects. The latter are readily discernible. Taken altogether, the books are too long; they tell us far more about the intricate shenanigans of the financial jungle than we ever wanted to know or could possibly absorb; and, even if everything that happens in Cowperwood's life is relevant, there still is too much of the relevant.

At the same time, the *Trilogy* undeniably possesses much of what a work of fiction must possess in order to endure: a life of its own. From its pages emerges a picture of American society as it existed during the Gilded Age at the turn of the twentieth century that is convincing beyond any question. For most of its length the *Trilogy* is dominated by the captivating figure of its larger-than-life hero. Dreiser had said that his chief purpose was to "draw [Cowperwood] as I see him. . . . And when I get through with him he'll stand there, unidealized and uncursed, for you . . . to take and judge according to your own lights and blindnesses and attitudes toward life."[11] The fact that many readers continue to find the portrait of Frank Cowperwood both engrossing and convincing explains why the *Trilogy* is considered to contain – after his masterworks, *Sister Carrie* and *An American Tragedy* – Dreiser's best work and most enduring contribution to American fiction.

Chapter Five

Self-portrait of the Artist: *The "Genius"*

Always the special individual, the genius of any kind, will be curbed and restrained if not actually pushed into the background.

Of all Dreiser's novels, *The "Genius"* has been the least praised and the most reviled. Upon its publication in 1915 reviewers found it to be "prodigiously long" and "Shapeless as a Philadelphia pie-woman," requiring more than 700 pages and 300,000 words to tell its story of a young artist from boyhood to middle age. The novel had its champions as well, of course, who received it as confirming evidence of Dreiser's mounting supremacy in the American realistic novel. One of these was Dreiser's fellow Chicagoan Ben Hecht. In his novel *Humpty Dumpty* (1924) Hecht portrays his young hero, Kent Savaron, as he moves into an apartment with his bride, arranging his books in a pair of bookcases. In the first bookcase, he explains, he will place books with enduring qualities, in the second those which disappoint. Among the writers relegated to bookcase number two are Balzac, Shaw, Wells, Galsworthy, D. H. Lawrence, and Sherwood Anderson. Bookcase number one is saved for such writers as Stephen Crane, H. L. Mencken, Ezra Pound, Dostoyevski, and James Joyce. On the shelf with this exalted company Savaron places *The "Genius,"* which he characterizes as "one of the most successful of the nine hundred and fifty thousand rewritings of Tom Jones."

But both in his own time and in ours, Ben Hecht has been outnumbered by critics who have found *The "Genius"* to be both overwritten and overlong. Considering the high hopes that its author held for it, this novel should have stood among Dreiser's master-works, yet readers usually find it less engrossing than *A Trilogy of*

Desire and considerably less compelling than *Sister Carrie*. Substantial blame for the book's relative failure can be attributed, at least in part, to the circumstances of its composition. Dreiser could weave fine work from the threads of his own life – as he repeatedly demonstrated – but to do so he needed to compose from a distance of time, a point of perspective from which real events might be assimilated into his larger experience and contemplated somewhat dispassionately. The best previous example of success via this method is the two- and three-decade lapse between his early boyhood experiences and their emergence in the fictional portraits of his father, mother, and family in *Jennie Gerhardt*. Dreiser also may have achieved a certain amount of objective distance by deliberately selecting an extrinsic subject (for example, Charles T. Yerkes); in this case, the compiling of sources, the mulling over, the selecting, and the formulating demanded a period of calendar time briefer than the autobiographical sources.

In writing *The "Genius"* Dreiser had the benefit of neither safeguard. Dealing with the most intimate and immediately personal material in any of his novels, he began putting pen to paper almost before the events he was describing had terminated. The story deals to a great extent with his childhood experiences, and Dreiser effectively re-creates such scenes; but *The "Genius"* also concentrates upon the period of his marriage and employment with the Butterick organization – roughly 1900 to 1910. Dreiser labored on the novel intermittently during these years and completed it in 1911 while *Jennie Gerhardt* was in press. Its autobiographical emphasis is prophetic of the method Thomas Wolfe later would adopt for such novels as *Look Homeward, Angel* and *You Can't Go Home Again*, and it exhibits the same weaknesses as Wolfe's work: a massive all-inclusiveness and a difficulty in imposing form and meaning on events recently transpired.

To structure his novel, Dreiser relied on experiences that had characterized his struggle toward a position of at least moderate affluence, groping always to locate his proper niche as literary artist. Having married with misgivings, he had seen that marriage fail from its inherent flaws. He had produced a work of art *(Sister Carrie)* and suffered a breakdown when that work was ill received. Seduced by the need for money into a passion for wealth, Dreiser attempted a union of business and art that in time proved incompatible. In *The*

"Genius" this same sequence of events controls the narrative, altered by only the most fragile veneer of fiction, with the story relying on theme and character to supply its unifying elements.

The theme is as powerful as any Dreiser dealt with, and he understood it well – artistic dedication in conflict with an unbridled personal sex drive and a rampantly materialistic society. The central character is Eugene Tennyson Witla, a painter who seeks a degree of artistic freedom that many might label as license. Character and theme can be strong supports in a novel. They have served to buttress many an otherwise sagging work of fiction, but in this case they do not manage to preserve *The "Genius"* from its flaws.

"The Perfection of Eighteen"

Helen Richardson Dreiser identifies the central figure of *The "Genius"* as a composite of the three men: verist painter Everett Shinn, a young art editor employed by the Butterick company, and Dreiser himself.[1] But it is apparent that the other two men are little more than tools for transmuting writer into painter and that Dreiser himself, slightly disguised, serves as the principal model for Eugene Tennyson Witla. The close correspondence between the life of Dreiser the man and Witla the character is strengthened by the knowledge that in his first attempt at writing *The "Genius"* Dreiser presented his hero not as a painter but as a newspaper reporter, as he himself had been during his twenties. Such correspondences between life and fiction continue, including the presentation of Dreiser's wife, Sara White, thinly disguised as Angela Blue.

In the novel, Eugene Witla emerges into young manhood in Alexandria, Illinois, an obscure hamlet on the prairies, akin to Dreiser's own Warsaw or Sullivan. At 17, not yet a painter, Eugene's artistic bent manifests itself through "an intense sense of beauty" that foreshadows the source of many of his later difficulties: "He admired girls – was mad about them – but only about those who were truly beautiful. . . . He invested them with more beauty than they had; the beauty was in his own soul. But he did not know that."[2]

For the next 750 pages, the reader observes Eugene lured toward emotional disaster by this "illusion," this "mirage" of beauty. Any beautiful girl whose manner suggests the most remote possibility of her being approachable can tumble Eugene off his precarious perch into an abyss of utter infatuation. When he is seventeen, it is Stella Appleton's "beauty like a tightened bow" that shoots love's barbs deep into his susceptible heart.

In rapid order a succession of girls succumb to Eugene's passion. Margaret Dunn, Ruby Kenny, Christina Channing, Frieda Roth, Carlotta Wilson, and Suzanne Dale are some of those dwelt upon in the story. But with the exception of Christina Channing, an opera singer, and Carlotta Wilson, a brash divorcée, each girl seems cast from the same mold. Eugene's loves are almost always 18 and possessed of the breathtaking loveliness of that age when girlhood blooms with "the sweetness of perfume of spring fires." Around these flames of perfect beauty Eugene flits like an excited moth, believing ever in the ultimate fulfillment of the mirage. But each happy illusion leads only to sad disillusion. Never relinquishing entirely his fruitless search for the one girl who will be his all-in-all, Eugene moves steadily toward stoicism and the very Dreiserian admission that "this is the way things are."

The tantalizing search for perfect beauty is accompanied, as it had been during Dreiser's young manhood, by a sharp dichotomy between art and business. This tug of war places Eugene between the opposed goals of fame and money, which Dreiser depicts as being mutually exclusive. Eugene Witla discovers that one cannot serve two masters, but he discovers it too late to avoid a sequence of violent personal – and career – reversals that place great strain upon credibility. Overnight, we are asked to believe, Eugene can plunge from being a fully productive artist to being a helpless neurotic. Inexplicably he passes from the threshold of considerable wealth to the basement of destitution. Dreiser writes of Witla: "He first gorged the spectacle of life and then suffered from mental indigestion." This describes the characteristic pattern of Witla's career. Prodded by his uncurbed appetites, the painter gluts upon his illusions. Meanwhile, Dreiser defends the right of the artist to absolute freedom and vehemently protests the cruelty of indifferent nature and the dark prejudices of a philistine society determined to curb creative genius.

The novel is divided into three books. The first, "Youth," parallels in part Dreiser's own early life, with the facts softened somewhat, as the boy's progress is traced from Alexandria to Chicago to New

York and as he is initiated into the spheres of art and sex. Because a young person's entry into Chicago had already been made much of in *Sister Carrie,* a reader of both novels is scarcely surprised to feel Eugene's youthful pulse race at discovering Chicago for the first time. Dreiser rises to the occasion with a Whitmanesque prose poem celebrating the growth of the midwestern industrial "magnet":

> This vast ruck of life that had sprung suddenly into existence upon the dank marshes of a lake shore. Miles and miles of dreary little houses; miles and miles of wooden block-paved streets, with gas lamps placed and water mains laid, and empty wooden walks set for pedestrians; the beat of a hundred thousand hammers; the ring of a hundred thousand trowels! Long, converging lines of telegraph poles; thousands upon thousands of sentinel cottages, factory plants, towering smoke stacks, . . . great broad highways of the tracks of railroads, ten, fifteen, twenty, thirty, laid side by side and strung with thousands upon thousands of shabby cars, like beads on a string. Engines clanging, trains moving, people watching at street crossings – pedestrians, wagon drivers, street car drivers, drays of beer, trucks of coal, brick, stone, sand – a spectacle of raw, necessary life! (*"Genius,"* 37)

Like other Dreiser protagonists, Eugene observes the conspicuous and almost sinful display of luxury in splendid clothes, fine homes, and all the other trappings of social prestige. He encounters also the despair, the shabbiness, and the gloom of squalor: "You could fail so easily. You could really starve if you didn't look sharp – the city quickly taught him that." Again, the observations are the mirror of Dreiser's own.

Eugene Witla inevitably discerns that life, despite its wonder, can be bitter as wormwood; that if one is to avoid persecution he must achieve some modus vivendi with the codes of convention; that money is the basis for all society's favors, every object and position being attached firmly to a price tag; that the individual means little enough to the universe at large and nothing at all to "the shifting, subtle forces of nature"; and that one is saved only by coming to an early and sobering realization that life is unfair. Eugene absorbs these lessons, just as his author had, but he could scarcely be described as being saved by learning them.

Book Two, "Struggle," opens upon the most fateful error in Eugene's life, one which plagues him for the rest of the book: his marriage to Angela Blue. In all important respects, this marriage tallies with Dreiser's to Sara White. The alliance is a mismating to which Dreiser-Witla agrees for all the wrong reasons: bowing to convention and to the opinions of others; marrying more out of duty or pity than love. Angela is older than Eugene. The bloom of 18 has passed, and she is earthbound, whereas he longs to soar the skies unfettered. Angela worships staid monogamy, while Eugene burns to dwell in an unconventional world created by his passions. Amid Eugene's bohemian company of artists and sophisticates, Angela is an oddity. Her few efforts to adjust prove her ineptitude. She flames with wild and self-defeating jealousy against every friend her husband cultivates.

Acknowledging in his heart that life is at bottom tragic, bitter, and deceptive, Eugene nevertheless manages to persuade himself that "there was happiness and peace in store for him probably. He and Angela would find it together living in each other's company, living in each other's embrace and by each other's kisses. It must be so. The whole world believed it – even he, after Stella and Margaret and Ruby and Angela. Even he" (*"Genius,"* 99).

If Eugene's marriage to Angela further complicates rather than solves his sexual problems by forcing him into a pretense of fidelity, so the couple's life in New York tears Eugene between artistic integrity and the gnawing desire to grab a share of the money whose presence tantalizes him. At this time, Eugene is 26. His art has brought him little return, either in dollars or in recognition. The feeling grows in him that, without fame, art is nothing – and that with fame, money will flow into his pockets: "He felt an eager desire to tear wealth and fame from the bosom of the world. Life must give him his share. If it did not he would curse it to his dying day" (*"Genius,"* 150). Of Eugene's burning desire for fame and wealth Dreiser can only reiterate: "The hope of fame – what hours of speculation, what pulses of enthusiasm, what fevers of effort, are based on that peculiarly subtle illusion!" (*"Genius,"* 222).

"Thank God for a Realist!"

At the studios of Kellner and Son, Eugene is granted his first one-man show of paintings. The canvases, as described in the novel, are a far cry from the romantic scenes popular at the time, for Dreiser guided Eugene's talent to correspond with his own realistic preferences in subject matter.

Wrenched from the streets of New York come painted scenes of industry and the lower classes: Fifth Avenue in a snowstorm, with unkempt, bony horses tugging a shabby bus along the snowswept streets[3]; Greeley Square in a drizzling rain, catching "the exact texture of seeping water on gray stones in the glare of various electric lights"; breadlines in which the destitute slouch like open sores on the body of society; milk trucks lumbering from the docks at four in the morning; an East Side pushcart street swarming with immigrant children. Eugene's pictures cry the same raucous tune that Dreiser's novels shouted to the world, the barbaric yawp first sounded in Walt Whitman's poems: "I'm dirty, I am commonplace, I am grim, I am shabby, but I am life."

"Thank God for a realist!" exclaims M. Charles, manager of Kellner and Son Gallery. But whether such shocking and grim paintings will sell is another question. Dreiser's novels had not been best-sellers, but Dreiser presents the exhibition of Eugene's verist paintings as achieving an unqualified success. Against the advice of a number of the critics, the obstinate public come to gaze and remain to buy. Feeling at last that he is crossing the threshold of a significant career, Eugene sails with Angela for Paris, where he plans to paint, paint, paint.

"A Sudden Glittering Light"

In the French capital Eugene suffers the first of the violent alterations that work against the believability of Dreiser's story. The sole foreshadowing of the precipitous tailspin into which Eugene hurtles comes at the end of a laudatory review that predicts a grand career for Eugene, with the cautionary proviso "if he perseveres, if his art does not fail him." *If his art does not fail him* – these seven syllables, we are told, haunt Eugene until, despite his prodigious output and his undeniable triumph in New York, abruptly "one day at his easel he was seized with a peculiar nervous disturbance – a sudden glittering light before his eyes, a rumbling in his ears, and a sensation that was as if his body were being pricked with ten million needles. It was as though his whole nervous system had given way at every minute point and division" (*"Genius,"* 250).

Some explanation of this emotional crack-up is called for, and Dreiser attempts one. He attributes much of the nervous breakdown

that incapacitates Eugene for five or six years to a "riot of indul-
gence" through which he and Angela have attempted, vainly, to save
their marriage. "He had," suggests the author, "no knowledge of the
effect of one's sexual life upon one's work, nor what such a life
when badly arranged can do to a perfect art."

To ask a reader to accept this nonsense is asking a good deal,
particularly when one considers Cowperwood, to whom sex was an
essential spur to the fullness of living. But it is asking much more to
believe it in the face of Dreiser's own life, which directly refutes most
everything he says about Eugene and sexual excess. In addition, by
presenting Eugene's breakdown with such abruptness and over-
simplification, Dreiser is asking too much by far.

Eugene Witla abandons art in an effort to recuperate from his
breakdown through hard work as a day laborer. Occupational therapy seems the remedy, although sexual abstinence apparently is not
a part of the prescription, for he continues to engage in sexual
affairs. When Angela discovers his duplicity, Eugene finds that "the
hells of love are bitter and complete," that revelation appears to
retard his recovery not at all. His composure regained, he is poised
for the struggle once more; he feels his talents on the rise again; and,
as an interim measure, he assumes a position on the advertising staff
of the New York *World*. This is the first step in a miraculous ascent
that seems to be even more headlong and unbelievable than his
breakdown.

Practically overnight, Eugene vaults from wages of $9 a week for
day labor on the railroad to a salary of $5,000 a year with the
Summerfield Advertising Agency. He goes from Summerfield's to
Kalvin Publishing at $8,000, then $12,000; to Swinton-Scudder-Davis
at $18,000, with swift promotion to $25,000. He is installed in a
white, blue, and gold office – rosewood desk and chairs, bouquets
in ornate vases – as managing publisher of United Magazine Corpo-
ration. Eugene is "making good" in a big way. He soon owns stocks
aggregating $30,000 and two lots in Montclair worth $6,000. The
prospect of a fortune dazzles him. In a little while – tomorrow, or
next year perhaps – he will liquidate his holdings, retire on his
profits, and return to his easel. But his first priority is to amass the
fortune that will make possible a new dedication to his painting.

Book 3, "Revolt," opens with Eugene traveling on the high road
to riches and loved by 18-year-old Suzanne Dale, daughter of a

friend of his employers.[4] He spies her first across the room at a reception that his wife, Angela, is giving. "With the irresistible attraction of an iron filing for a magnet," says Dreiser, he is drawn to her, and she to him.

Oval-faced, radiantly healthy, ripe-lipped, and with chestnut hair curling above blue-gray eyes, Suzanne, to Eugene, puts to shame the glory of dew-sprinkled roses: "If he could only, once more in his life, have the love of a girl like that!" Although he realizes that taking Suzanne as his lover will constitute an adventure of maximum hazard, the illusion of love is so powerful that he is ready, even eager, to wager all for love. Wife, position, money lose all meaning. Only Suzanne counts. "For the first time in his life he was to have a woman after his own heart, so young, so beautiful, so intellectual, so artistic. With Suzanne by his side, he was about to plumb the depths of all the joys of living."

For a time, paradise seems well within reach. "Surely the gods were good. What did they mean? To give him fame, fortune and Suzanne into the bargain?" In a Dreiser novel? Hardly. The dazzling light of Suzanne Dale blinds Eugene to the antagonistic forces bent upon thwarting his hopes. In an attempt to bind her husband to her, Angela conceives a child. Suzanne's mother discovers Suzanne's liaison with Eugene and spirits her daughter away to Canada, but not before informing Eugene's employers of his actions, which to them constitute an unforgivable impropriety. Still blindly confident of Suzanne's adoration, Eugene sacrifices for this mirage the position that has made his investments possible – and he is stripped of both fortune and love. Suzanne is soon persuaded that mother knows best; she is brought to realize that the chemism of her makeup had caused her to "make a fool of herself with Eugene." The lamp of illusion, stubborn as it is, is eventually extinguished. Angela dies in childbirth, leaving the "Genius" with a daughter to raise and the faint possibility of a slow, rational return to the art from which he should never have strayed.

Piecing together the shards of his life, Eugene leaps from one belief to another in a search for meaning. For a time Christian Science seems the answer. Then he becomes convinced the world is ruled by a devil, "a Gargantuan Brobdingnagian Mountebank" of malicious intent. He at last arrives at the position his author had outlined in "The Equation Inevitable," a state described as "not of

abnegation, but of philosophic open-mindedness or agnosticism."
Observing the universe, the human being shrinking smaller than a
mote among swirling galaxies of stars, amid the confusing play and
interplay of cosmic forces, who was to know what to believe? Apparently nature permitted anything in life; nothing remained stationary.
"Perhaps life loved only change, equation, drama, laughter." In this
huge chaotic system called life the individual came and went, acting
his tiny part in the drama, stung with delight by favorable illusions,
crushed by the vagaries of circumstance, and able to alter nothing in
the system itself, which remained as before – fixed, inscrutable, and
eternal.

"A Band of Wasp-like Censors"

The "Genius" may not have been top-drawer Dreiser, but it did
provoke a number-one battle with the censors, official and unofficial.
The smog of trouble had hung in the air since the winter of 1914
when Harper's, having printed The Titan and brought the volume to
the binding stage, abruptly informed Dreiser that it was being withdrawn from publication. It has been speculated that the fictional
portrait of Emilie Grigsby (the model for Berenice in the novel) was
so obviously drawn from life that her powerful friends pressured
Harper's into suppressing the book. Whatever the case, Dreiser
found himself facing a repetition of the Doubleday attempt to
suppress Sister Carrie in 1900. This time, rather than insisting upon
his contractual rights, he went searching for a publisher with fortitude enough to see the book onto the stalls. Most publishers
declined, but finally John Lane and Company, after considerable
debate and soul-searching, accepted The Titan and published it in
1914 without much sign of adverse reaction.

Reassured, Lane the following year issued The "Genius,"
although not without misgivings concerning its highly controversial
subject matter and treatment. If The Titan had seemed too realistic
for America's major houses to risk purveying, then surely The
"Genius," with its more explicit presentation of the erotic and its
harsher indictment of American society, might expect to be met with
an outcry. Indeed the Little Review, after hailing the book, declared
"a howl will go up" from the critics and printed imaginative prophe-
cies of the book's damnation as "sensually depraved and degener-

ate," as "striking at the bed rock of public solidarity, of home happiness, of everything decent and worth while."[5] That prediction came true.

In July 1916, the New York Society for the Suppression of Vice launched its attack upon *The "Genius."* Founded in 1873 by Anthony Comstock, this organization had amassed an impressive record in purging the country of obvious pornography, after which it turned its guns on the classics, banning, expurgating, and attacking. Authors such as Rabelais, Boccaccio, Shakespeare, Swift, Balzac, Zola, and Hardy came under fire. *Jude the Obscure* was banned; *Leaves of Grass* was condemned. But Dreiser's novel was the first major work of an American contemporary to be threatened. In New York, John S. Sumner, successor to Anthony Comstock, confronted the John Lane Company with "75 lewd and 17 profane passages" in the novel. Ordering them deleted, Summer frightened the publisher into withdrawing the book temporarily.

Dreiser suggested an immediate counterattack. "A fight is the only thing and I want Lane to fight," he wrote his good friend H. L. Mencken. The plates of the book, to prevent their being seized and destroyed, were shipped out of the state. The United States postal authorities had been appealed to by the Comstock society and, under threat of the book's being banned from the mail, Dreiser wrote Mencken of his intention to force the issue by mailing a copy personally. He declared he was "perfectly willing to break the postal laws and go to jail myself. It will save my living expenses this winter" (Elias 1959, 1:221).

To newspaper reporters Dreiser was vociferous. "If my name were Dreiserevsky," he growled, "and I said I came from Moscow I'd have no trouble. But I come from Indiana – so goodnight!" Mencken worked tirelessly in his friend's behalf, circulating leaflets and letters until 478 signatures had been obtained, many of them from authors or critics who signed to defend the principle of freedom of expression even while deploring that a major censorship battle must concern a book they felt not to be fully defensible.

Dreiser's next step, since his publishers had not mustered the courage to reissue the novel as he felt they had promised, was to bring a friendly suit against the John Lane Company for failing to fulfill contract stipulations. The case was heard in May 1918 before the Appellate Division of the Supreme Court and was strongly argued by both defendant and plaintiff. "FIVE JUDGES WILL DECIDE IF *THE 'GENIUS'* IS GENIUS, TOMMYROT, OR PLAIN FILTH" was the headline featured by the Brooklyn *Daily Eagle*. The five judges of the Appellate Court, apparently not sufficiently impressed by the 478 signatures and a supportive cable from English writers presented by the defense, refused to rule for Dreiser.

For five more years, until Horace Liveright had the courage to republish it, the novel stayed off the market; yet the battle, seemingly a defeat, was in actuality the first stage of victory. By awakening authors and critics to the inherent threats against literary freedom and by acquainting the public with the issues involved in suppression, the case of *The "Genius"* broke the ice for more favorable decisions to follow – as in the *Jurgen* trial of 1919 and the *Ulysses* trial of 1934. Slowly the tide of public sympathy shifted sufficiently to uphold freedom of literary expression.

Chapter Six

"Society Should Ask Forgiveness":
An American Tragedy

"The Way Life Has Organized Itself"

In Herkimer County, New York, in 1906 a young man named Chester
Gillette found his pregnant sweetheart to be an intolerable barrier to
his hopes for rising in the world, lured her with the prospect of a
lovers' outing to Big Moose Lake, and drowned her. The victim's
name was Grace Brown, and her murderer was almost immediately
discovered, apprehended, tried, convicted, and executed. The crime
was not unique. It closely paralleled a number of other murder cases
that had been covered in American newspapers, including that of
Carlisle Harris, whose involvement with a poor girl threatened his
marriage to a girl of wealth.

Theodore Dreiser thought he heard a familiar note running
through these cases. There was a thread of similarity he had been
aware of ever since his early newspaper days, a pattern that might
serve admirably as the framework for an important novel. Dreiser
recognized something distinctly (and frighteningly) *American* about
the nature of the murders, and he studied a group of these
"American tragedies" before he decided that the circumstances of
the Gillette-Brown murder were ideally suited to the book he wanted
to produce.

Abstracted, the murders followed lines that might be predicted
with near-scientific exactness, and their significance tallied rather
well with Dreiser's own notions of an American society that had
become materialist to the core, glittering with blandishments for the
young and encouraging them to pursue "the dream of success" at all
cost.

In the existing system, where wealth had become the sole object
of human endeavor, society itself played the villain's role, or so it

appeared to Dreiser. Society built irresistibly enticing parks where green thoughts might be contemplated in a green shade; then it spiked the sward with KEEP OFF THE GRASS signs. Young America had been nurtured on tales of the office boy who rose toward status and wealth by marrying the boss's daughter. Dreiser himself had employed a variation of this theme in *Sister Carrie,* wherein men of steadily higher station ease the heroine's ascent to wealth and fame.

For a young man the problem differed. Not only were a man's chances for a wealthy marriage infinitesimal compared to the Cinderella possibilities open to a girl possessed of beauty and charm, but when the young man had gotten himself inextricably involved with a poor girl, his difficulties multiplied. He soon discovered that such a girl could do very little to advance his career. But what if the girl then found herself pregnant? Supposing that this situation were compounded by the young man's simultaneously catching a glimmer of hope for a romance with an heiress, frustration might build to explosive proportions. If the pregnant sweetheart should refuse to be set aside, murder might easily be the result; and often, Dreiser noticed, it was.

The illusory but widely accepted American notion that an ambitious boy may rise to wealth with comparative ease seemed to Dreiser a primal cause of such crimes. Once again life seemed to illustrate graphically the intense and cruel attraction that wealth exerted on the young. The power of the "money ideal" could easily overwhelm those who were poor. Continued observation, for Dreiser, merely underscored the truth of his concept of man as a being whose feet are in the trap of circumstance and whose eyes are on an illusion. Dreiser was certain that for most, the dream of power, wealth, and luxury had no more substance than a mirage; and *Mirage* became the working title under which he began writing.

A Tree Grows in Union Square

Precisely when Dreiser first contemplated writing *An American Tragedy* is difficult to establish, but certainly, as with his other books, the idea teased his mind long before he wrote it. "I carry my plots around with me year after year before setting pen to paper," he answered an interrogator. "By the time I am ready to write I see the book as plainly as if it were a tree rising up before my eyes. Root, trunk, branches, twigs, so to speak, are all there; it is only the leaves that require to be sketched in" (Dudley, 409-10).

The "sketching in" of the *Tragedy*'s foliage was under way by 1922.[1] Dreiser in 1919 had met a distant cousin of his, Helen Richardson, who recently had been divorced from her first husband. Tumbling head over heels in love with her, he followed her the next year to Hollywood. Theatrically ambitious, she began a career in films as an extra and eventually established a minor career as a "starlet" in such pictures as *The Flame of Youth* and *The Four Horsemen of the Apocalypse*. Still officially married, though estranged from his wife for a decade, Dreiser persuaded Helen to be his. Thus began the most permanent sexual relationship in his life, an affair that still was not unmarked by jealousy and stormy separation. Eventually – but not for another 20 years – they married.

By 1922 Dreiser's desire to complete *Mirage* was overriding. With 20 chapters written, Dreiser could not rest until the skeletal tree in his mind was leafed out with words and the book was seen through the press. In October he and Helen left California for New York. The following summer the two drove northward into Herkimer County where, 17 years earlier, the murder of Grace Brown had occurred. In Dreiser's novel, Grace was renamed Roberta Alden and Chester Gillette became Clyde Griffiths.

Already at Dreiser's disposal were the official court records of the Gillette trial and sheaves of newspaper reports dating from the time of the trial and Gillette's execution. But he wanted to view the area at first hand. In preparing *The Financier,* he had dogged Charles T. Yerkes's trial to Philadelphia, Chicago, New York, and Europe. Now, stopping in Cortland, New York, which was to become the Lycurgus of his novel, Dreiser toured the various sections of that small city to obtain a firm impression of the locale: the residential area in which he would locate Wykeagy Avenue, home of the wealthy Griffiths; the factory section where the collar factory might feasibly be located; the middle- and lower-class regions where Mrs. Cuppy's boardinghouse and Roberta Alden's lonely room would be located. Near the hamlet of South Otselic – to become Blitz, Roberta's home in the book – Dreiser and Helen drove down the dusty road that had led to Grace Brown's country home, to be described vividly in the novel when Clyde Griffiths stops there by accident and is obliged to request road information from Titus Alden.

Finally, there were the Adirondack sites, the villages of Old Forge (Gun Lodge in the book) and Big Moose Lake, the scene of the crime, which Dreiser was to rename Big Bittern. Here he and Helen rowed out on the water, drifting into quiet, isolated, tree-lined inlets, any one of which might conceivably have supplied the remote depths into which Roberta sank and from which Clyde escaped dripping and panic-stricken.

After working through the summer in a lake-district cabin, Dreiser and Helen returned to New York and Dreiser took an office in the Guardian Life Building near Union Square where he could continue his task without interruption. Two friends, J. G. Robin and Arthur Carter Hume, tenants in the same building, were equipped to supply him with technical information concerning points of law in the trial scenes of his book, and he drew on them both.

Time was growing short. A great deal of writing had already gone into the *Tragedy* manuscript, but much more was to be done. The mass of paper was beginning to shape up into a fascinating story, and Dreiser gave his undivided attention to completing it. Of his work during these days, Helen Dreiser wrote that "he was like a sculptor working on a figure which had grown so large that he seemed to be throwing his clay high to the top with a mighty hand. He modeled, chiseled, formed and reformed until one could see and feel the whole structure coming to life. There was so much mass material and so much modeling to be done before it was acceptable to him – writing, rewriting, revising, four, five or six times" (H. Dreiser, 110). It was 1925 now, and still Dreiser was writing. His publisher, Liveright, was clamoring for the final manuscript. Early sections of the book were already being set up in type, and proofs were being circulated privately among selected readers. Tentative opinions began coming in. Some readers damned, some praised. Some questioned the title, which Dreiser had changed from *Mirage* to *An American Tragedy*. "How in the world can Dreiser call a book *An American Tragedy?*" asked Thomas Smith, Liveright's closest literary adviser. But the author held firm, feeling that he had located the only title that could express his deeply held convictions concerning the peculiarly American quality of his novel.

By November all was accomplished but the polishing of the final chapters. For these pages Dreiser hoped to confirm his rendering of the death house scenes by visiting execution row in Sing Sing prison.

He must be certain of his facts, rely as little as possible upon others' eyes, others' words. How many cells in a death block? Arranged in what number of tiers? What were the dimensions of a condemned man's cell? How furnished? What color its walls? How thick a door, and how fashioned? Of what nature the inmates? Details, details, details, and each one, to the writer, vitally important. With Mencken's aid in arranging a visit to the death house at Sing Sing, the novelist obtained his facts regarding executions and pressed ahead to the conclusion of his novel.

On 15 November 1925, Dreiser completed *An American Tragedy*. He was satisfied to put the final pages of manuscript in the hands of his publisher, while he and Helen at once set out on a motor tour of the eastern coast, heading for Florida and what they hoped might be their long-deserved rest.

The Tree in Foliage

What was the nature of the manuscript Horace Liveright received from Dreiser and hurried onto the bookstalls before the year was out? Its massiveness might be its first impact upon a reviewer. Lengthy volumes were expected from Dreiser, but this was far longer than any single novel he had produced. It was so lengthy even after considerable cutting that it was sectioned off into three discrete "books" totaling some 840 pages and was issued in two volumes at the unusual price of $5 a set.

Readers of *An American Tragedy* were offered the birth-to-death chronicle of an American boy with much the same basic aspirations, the same dream of success, that Frank Cowperwood had dreamed, yet devoid of so much as an ounce of the great financier's capacity to succeed.

Dreiser had taken care to make Clyde Griffiths as much as circumstances permit an "average" American. That is, the extremes of hereditary influence were avoided, leaving the boy neither the mentally crippled deviate of Dreiser's drama *The Hand of the Potter* nor the squid-devouring lobster of *The Financier*. Clyde stands on middle ground; he is a young man for whom many fates are possible, depending on circumstances. What happens to Clyde will happen not only because of the drives (desires, Dreiser would label them) with which he has been naturally endowed; the influences that mold him and the direction from which the indifferent winds of chance blow upon him will also be critical determinants of his fate.

From the Door of Hope to the Green-Davidson

The first book of *An American Tragedy* lays a foundation for the structure to follow H. L. Mencken thought the detailed story of Clyde's boyhood too long, too involved – in all, a great mistake. But, on the contrary, the sheer weight of detail elaborating Clyde's boyhood is precisely what is needed to buttress the actions of books 2 and 3, making credible – even predictable – Clyde's actions in the love triangle at the heart of the book. Without the first book and the additions Dreiser later makes to the story of the murder, the central plot might strike a reader as being contrived and somewhat pat. But as it is, the careful and extensive foreshadowing in the first book casts a long shadow, creating such a great sense of probability that Clyde's later actions come not as a surprise but as a fulfillment.

It is largely this detailing of environmental pressures at all stages of Clyde's story that allows the novel to escape from becoming a mere transcript of the Gillette trial and therefore just another "fictionalized" version of a sordid crime. The first book is invented in its entirety by Dreiser. Although it does not deal at all with the crime and introduces only one of the figures in the love triangle on which the central story depends, its mass of detail establishes Clyde's personality with such precision that a reader can predict the boy's reactions to later events with considerable accuracy. By the end of book 1, we know Clyde's hopes, dreams, and ambitions. We also know Clyde's limitations, blindnesses, and fears. We have seen how a carrot dangled before Clyde's hungry eyes will stimulate him and set him leaping; and we have seen that a crisis will trigger Clyde to rush for escape.

Essentially pagan in nature, Clyde even at the age of 12 is moved to rebel against the rigidly moral street-mission environment inhabited by his parents. His humiliation deepens each time he is dragged through the streets to sing with the volunteer group from the Door of Hope Mission run by his father and mother. He is poor as the proverbial church mouse, yet he is vain and proud as well. He echoes the spirit of young Dreiser's refrain "No common man am I." And he finds himself stifling in the fetid atmosphere of Bickel Street:

"The whole neighborhood was so dreary and run-down that he hated the thought of living in it." The desperate reluctance to be trapped and the corresponding blind scrambling for escape that characterize his later life are planted in Clyde from this age.

What happens to children from such a family, such an environment, when their little mission world collides with the great unfeeling universe beyond its walls? The oldest girl in the family, Esta, reminiscent of Dreiser's own sisters, is seduced through "chemic witchery" by an actor and then deserted, pregnant. The episode heightens the contradiction Clyde has already sensed between the God of his parents – the Good Shepherd who cares for His flock – and the uncaring, matter-of-fact way of the world. Clyde himself is increasingly magnetized by the attractions of the forbidden streets. A glance in the mirror proves he is not bad-looking. And he soon discovers (like Carrie Meeber) what others regard as desirable: money, position, clothes. "If only he had a better coat, a nicer shirt, finer shoes, a good suit, a swell overcoat like some boys had!"

At 15, Clyde regards his job as soda clerk in a third-rate drug store as the ultimate measure of success, but before long he sets his sights on a more glamorous target. From soda clerk he graduates to bellboy at the Green-Davidson Hotel. By his standards handsomely uniformed and magnificently paid, he is free for the first time to set his own hours for returning home. He could stay out till midnight if he desired! To what greater glories could a young man aspire? And the hotel itself – the very sight of that massive tower of brick and green marble makes Clyde tremble with excitement. Within its walls he rubs shoulders with the wealth and display of the world. He learns also the delights and duplicities of sex. As a whole, the hotel serves as a symbol of the world that Clyde's nature starves for. The mission and the hotel: these two structures dominate the first book of the novel and provide Clyde with his ineffectual, misguided "education." In one way or another, their influence is felt on every page of the novel.

From Thorpe Street to Wykeagy Avenue

Clyde flees from Kansas City following an automobile accident that kills a pedestrian. By now, panic and flight have been established as his characteristic methods of meeting a crisis. By coincidence he encounters his wealthy uncle Asa Griffiths in Chicago. But after moving to Lycurgus and a position with the Griffiths Collar and Shirt Company, the boy is stalemated once again. As in Kansas City, he hovers between two worlds, poor and rich. The polarity between the mission and the hotel is repeated.

Older now, going on 21, Clyde has managed to inch upward in the world. But he will always be a fumbler and a groper. Despite Clyde's hope of social acceptance, his uncle's snobbish family rebuffs him because of indifference and because of his chance resemblance to his rather vain cousin Gilbert, who resents having a "double." Clyde's social world in Lycurgus is bounded by the four walls of Mrs. Cuppy's boardinghouse on Thorpe Street.

Being a Griffiths – even though only a shirt-tail relative – allows Clyde to feel superior to his coworkers at the factory. They defer to him, conscious of his difference from the ordinary employee. Yet, for all the notice his relatives take of Clyde, the Griffiths mansion on "that beautiful Wykeagy Avenue" might as well display a NO ADMIT-TANCE sign on its gateway. He is neither a common worker nor an owner, and his anomalous position is frustrating. Out of it, with an inevitability of circumstance, grows the tragedy of his life.

Feeling almost certain that the socially-prominent Griffiths mean to exclude him forever from their private lives, yet never quite giving up hope altogether, Clyde drifts into a clandestine affair with Roberta Alden that results in her pregnancy. At somewhat the same time comes his chance encounter with the society belle Sondra Finchley. She uses him at first to irritate his cousin Gilbert. Then Clyde enjoys a flurry of popularity with the "set," and he becomes infatuated with Sondra. Finally, incomprehensibly, he feels that he is in love – or what passes for love. It seems that the closed door to Clyde's dream of success is swinging wide at last.

On Sondra's insistence, the Griffiths family is goaded into accepting Clyde. Once this happens, his future teems with promise. He envisions a grand future for himself: wealth, luxury, position; life in a mansion on Wykeagy Avenue. This is his unreal dream. On the level of reality, the picture darkens. Roberta, sensing herself trapped, fights to preserve herself. Clyde finds her petulant and somewhat vengeful. Because of her conventional rearing and Clyde's own promises to her, she insists that Clyde marry her. Thus, it is that just as Sondra opens the door to affluence and invites Clyde to enter, Roberta pulls it shut. The frustration is intolerable.

Murder is the method Clyde chooses to gain entry to a life on Wykeagy Avenue. But the novel stands at a far remove from the conventional murder mystery. Because Clyde's own ineptitude provides the police with every necessary clue to ensure his discovery, the question is not *whether* he will be caught but only *when*. And it is here that the mass of details in the first book bears fruit; for Clyde, having determined his modus operandi, performs now in precisely the manner one has been led to expect. This fact enhances the action with an inevitability that neither shocks nor surprises but, instead, gratifies a preconceived notion of who and what Clyde, another "waif amid forces," might be.

The great point in Dreiser's *Tragedy* is that a reader, loathing Clyde's motives and his methods, can still understand and sympathize with the boy in his predicament, as Dreiser slowly and exactingly dramatizes Clyde's bootless fumbling for a solution. He takes Roberta to a physician in hopes of obtaining an abortion, but the doctor refuses to perform the procedure. He searches out every nostrum he can find in an effort to rid himself of the child. Nothing works. At last he sends Roberta to her home in Blitz and does his utmost to wipe the entire experience out of his memory.

I. A. Richards has said of tragedy that "suppressions and sublimations alike are devices by which we endeavor to avoid issues which might bewilder us. The essence of tragedy is that it forces us to live for a moment with them." This surely is Clyde's position. Threatening to expose him, Roberta obstinately refuses to evaporate from Clyde's life. Clyde is forced at last to face that fact squarely. Either he must marry Roberta voluntarily and discard his dreams of affluence or he must abandon her and see his hopes die. The former he is constitutionally unable to do. The latter he cannot allow to happen.

If he cannot untangle the Gordian knot, perhaps he can sever it. Clyde has always been the plaything of chance, and once again coincidence provides his answer. He reads the newspaper report of an accidental tragedy on a nearby lake. A young couple, enjoying an outing, drown when their boat overturns. Suddenly he knows what must be done and how he will do it. But even having arrived at his decision, Clyde is temperamentally unfit to perpetrate the deed in cold blood. The extended scenes preliminary to the drowning of Roberta are prolonged by Clyde's vacillation, his nervous bungling, his decision and indecision. They masterfully produce the effect Dreiser was grasping for. Stalling, searching for time, deciding and reconsidering, Clyde wanders with Roberta from lake to lake, ostensibly searching for the ideal honeymoon spot, but actually seeking the seclusion appropriate to a bloody deed – and the courage to kill.

The death scene itself is neatly balanced between guilt and innocence. On the still waters of Big Bittern two young people are at last alone – but for divergent reasons. The shoreline is deserted. The wooded inlets are dark with trees. So far as one can tell, no peering eyes can witness. Clyde hears the harsh, unearthly cry of the weir-weir bird: "Kit, kit, kit, c-a-a-ah!" Roberta prattles innocently about her "Clydie Mydie" and about the new collar factory in Syracuse where he may find employment after they are married. Clyde, tense as a fiddle string, anticipates the perfect moment to kill, yet delays, shrinking from the deed. He is paralyzed. A "chemic revulsion" repels him from the very notion of murder, yet a violent impulse urges him to seize the moment and implement his plan. His nerves are riddled. He squats in a trance, staring at Roberta in a "static between a powerful compulsion to do and yet not to do."

Then Roberta rises from her seat in the stern of the boat and shatters the counterpoise. Instantaneously the fatal chain of events recommences. The drowning occurs roughly as Clyde had originally planned, with the difference that now it is initiated not by him but by events. Clyde has relinquished freedom of choice, and chance takes control. To increase doubt concerning Clyde's guilt, Dreiser not only arranges Roberta's chance movement but also puts into the young man's hand a camera rather than the tennis racket actually wielded by Chester Gillette. A camera, after all, is a rather natural accoutrement for a boat ride and picnic along the shore of a picturesque lake. As Roberta reaches for Clyde's hand, she tips the boat. Clyde's bodily reflexes, conditioned as they now are by tension and pressures, cause him to repulse her. Struck accidentally by his camera, she falls into the lake.

Roberta drowns. Clyde, having failed – out of panic or deliberately? – to answer her single cry for help, crawls dripping up onto the dark shore. In his mind is "the thought that, after all, he had not really killed her."

Or had he? He had meant to, originally. Yet he had not actually pushed her into the lake. That seems more her own doing. Nor had he guided the gunwale of that boat and made it strike her skull. Yet he had neglected to rescue her when he might have. But in her frenzy she might have impeded his own survival, dragged him down with her.

Is he guilty or innocent? Even Clyde does not know for sure.

From Big Bittern to Murderers' Row

The final book of *An American Tragedy* bears toward its conclusion like a boulder crashing downhill, impelled by the momentum of all that has gone before. Dreiser's eye is always on the mark. There is no faltering, no groping for ways and means, no doubt about what he is doing. Each incident is probed, each scene developed with the same thorough documentation that lent verisimilitude to the first two books. But so deftly and even rhythmically is it all paced – the clipped narrative style of the trial scenes, repeating "And then . . . and then . . . " – and so crucially is each segment made to bear on the total structure that few readers feel that the progress of the story is impeded.

The verdict against Clyde can easily be predicted even before the prolonged trial has gotten under way. But it makes for exciting reading nevertheless. A tonnage of irrefutable circumstantial evidence is at the disposal of the district attorney. One by one, material objects from Clyde's past are entered to confront him. His camera is dredged from the lake, and his tripod is found where he hid it in the woods as he fled in panic from Big Bittern to Twelfth Lake and his beloved Sondra. Roberta's clothing is displayed and her pitiful letters are recited aloud in court for the tears they evoke. As a climax, the boat, the identical vessel from which Roberta tumbled into the dark waters, is shown to the jury. Each exhibit entered by the prosecution binds Clyde to the victim or to the death scene and helps to establish motive and opportunity. In support of these comes the testimony of innkeepers, lawmen, guides, physicians – the condemning words of 127 witnesses in all. To stand against the force of these there is little more than the bewilderment and confusion of

Clyde, who is never certain whether he should be labeled a murderer or a victim of circumstances.

The total effect of book 3 is one of dazzling virtuosity and skill. It is Dreiser at his very best. So many things are to be kept in sight and under control. The mise en scène, the wider landscape, must be continued lest the American ambiance of the title be lost in the particularities of Clyde's trial. What of the wealthy Griffiths, who feel that Clyde has betrayed them, who feel also that they have betrayed themselves and their circle by ever accepting Clyde into their lives? Social pressure demands that they make at least the gesture of obtaining an attorney for him. Paradoxically they appear to defend the boy and to cut themselves off from him simultaneously.

And what of the Finchleys, in whose little vacuum-cleaner empire Clyde dreamed of becoming an executive by marriage? While Clyde and Roberta, being poor, have their lives stripped naked to the public glare, the Finchleys can escape in anonymity to Narraganset. Sondra, through the influence of wealth and power, is known only as "Miss X." Her true identity is shielded from the newspapers, played down by the trial attorneys. Powerful forces, both economic and political, are at work determining who shall be exposed, who protected – and money, position, and influence are the major determinants.

The idea of the distribution of guilt has been quietly worked into the novel from its first pages, but it rises to the surface every now and then like a fish leaping from still waters. Doctor Glenn, whom Roberta consults in hope of obtaining an abortion, piously lectures her on medical ethics. There are, he admits, doctors here and there "who take their professional ethics a little less seriously than I do; but I cannot let myself become one of them." But even as he dismisses Roberta with this sermon, he is conscious of having a number of times in the recent past performed abortions for "young girls of good family who had fallen from grace and could not otherwise be rescued." *Of good family* is the key phrase; it means, of course, families of wealth and social status. Self-interest still rules society.

As for Clyde's attorneys, the firm of Belknap and Jephson retained by Samuel Griffiths, they lend patient ears to Clyde's story. But their hardheaded practical experience leads them to reject his tale as an impossibility in terms of legal defense. In its place they concoct a plea of insanity or "brain storm," which they deem a possibility for saving Clyde's life. This option is summarily rejected by the wealthy Griffiths because in its wider ramifications it might threaten to taint their own family line. The Darwinian aspects of the story are readily apparent here. An unambiguous struggle for survival is under way. Everyone has himself to protect. No one really cares – or can afford to care – about Clyde.

The reintroduction of Clyde's mother, Elvira Griffiths, is a masterful stroke on Dreiser's part. Not only does it signify the degree of national interest aroused by the trial – the Asa Griffiths are operating a mission in far-off Denver when they are hunted out by the newspapers and used for headline fodder – but it also neatly ties the end of Dreiser's story to its beginning pages and lends a satisfying unity to the novel, bringing the action full circle. Of course, the mother's final struggle to save her son from the electric chair is no more effectual than her earlier struggle to preserve him from the corrupting taint of materialism. The world, having lured Clyde into transgression, now exacts its tribute; and Clyde dies more bewildered than ever.

So long as American society persists in organizing itself the way it has, Dreiser appears to be cautioning his reader, the American tragedies he portrayed in every one of his novels will be doomed to repeat themselves.

"I've Hit the Mark This Time"

Dreiser used all of his novels to dramatize the beliefs and lessons of his lifetime, but the volume that does the job most thoroughly and with greatest skill is *An American Tragedy*. In it, not only are Dreiser's novelistic shortcomings reduced to their minimum, but the single story blends the author's various attitudes harmoniously. Here, for instance, the reader glimpses again the Dreiser childhood, less detailed yet still recognizable. Here the world of poverty is squared off once more against the world of wealth. Once again, peering through closed windows into illuminated parlors from which he is excluded, is the lone outsider, by this time a hallmark of Dreiser's novels. Here too is the seduction of the young and the yearning by material fascinations. Throughout, as always, the winds of chance whip capriciously, unjustly, disastrously. Sex remains an irresistible force dominating man, submerging him in illusions that lead, in this case, not to mismating alone but to catastrophe. *An American Tragedy* actually contains nothing that is wholly new to Dreiser's notion of life, yet it weaves together every main thread of his philosophy into a single finished fabric.

The reception of Dreiser's novel is a valid measure of the changing attitudes toward fiction between 1900 and 1925, changes Dreiser had labored a quarter of a century to influence. All the points made in the novel had been made previously, but Dreiser had been ignored, attacked, suppressed, and banned for making them. How this new book would be received he did not know. Surely he hoped for the best, but his past experience could scarcely have led him to expect a resounding ovation. After all, in its pages the structure of American society itself was attacked; the book's readers would find themselves portrayed as participants in a tragic situation of immense proportions.

When the nation proved to be as "ready" for *An American Tragedy* as it had been unprepared for *Sister Carrie,* the irony of the affair could not have helped but strike Dreiser as further corroboration of the inscrutable ways in which life turned. With surprising unanimity the critics spoke out in praise. H. G. Wells termed the book "one of the very greatest novels of this century." Joseph Wood Krutch called it "the great American novel of our generation." Even Stuart P. Sherman, inimical to all of Dreiser's previous works, performed a complete about-face and bestowed his highest praise: the book was *moral.* The novel was banned in Boston, to be sure, but the power of the vice crusaders had been broken and the opposition did not spread.

To find himself so defended by the critics was almost as odd for Dreiser as to have his writings bought and read on a wholesale basis. He had produced, for him, a genuine anomaly – a best-seller! In Florida, where he had gone for relaxation and instead had been sucked into the great land boom, joining the rest of *boobus Americanus* in purchasing exorbitantly priced lots that soon would be swept out to sea with the tides, Dreiser remarked to Helen, "Well, it looks as if I've hit the mark this time. I think I'll go back home and collect some of the spoils" (H. Dreiser, 120).

And spoils there were in abundance. Within a year, the *Tragedy* had sold out seven editions and was being read everywhere. Dramatized, it played to packed houses in America and abroad. Soon arrived the ultimate accolade, the most genuine symbol of the world's acceptance – a bid from the motion pictures. Paramount's Famous Players wanted his book for the screen. How much was he going to ask for the rights? His publisher, with a heavy stake in the prospective sale, was anxious to close the deal. A flat $100,000, said Dreiser. Impossible! $25,000, possibly. At the very top, $35,000. A man must be realistic, after all. Dismayed that the negotiations he had launched might founder upon a request of such astronomical proportions, Horace Liveright made every attempt to dissuade Dreiser from demanding the full amount; but Dreiser held firm. This was his chance, and he meant to make the most of it. Taking the deal into his own hands, he met the head of Famous Players, Jesse Lasky, in a luncheon conference and emerged with a contract for $90,000.

Overnight Dreiser became, by his standards, a man of wealth; he had "arrived" and the spoils were his. Now well known, he became a much-discussed public figure; he was in demand as a speaker, and he was interviewed for his views on the American system, on writing, finance, marriage and divorce, and capital punishment. Visiting Europe again, in 1926, he was accepted as an authority on anything American. The Soviets, aware of his growing sympathy for the Communist experiment then rounding out its first decade, invited him to tour their nation. He did so, admiring a number of their industrial accomplishments and social reforms. Yet he returned home not fully persuaded that the Soviets had produced paradise on earth, as was their claim.[2] His career went well. Stories, articles, and books flowed in an increasing stream. Magazines, which in recent years had shown considerable reluctance to publish his work, now clamored for anything they might rush into print.

A Thorn in the Rose

All this glory was not without its disappointment. The Pulitzer Prize for 1925, which Dreiser surely coveted for *An American Tragedy* and probably deserved, went instead to Sinclair Lewis. Dreiser must have thought it ironic that the apprentice should be honored while the master was neglected, but he remained silent. While he could not have but admired, even applauded, Lewis's audacity in refusing the prize, his own failure to win this recognition cut sharply into wounds left by old rejections. Those wounds were reopened in 1930 when the Swedish Academy decided at last to award the Nobel Prize to an American. He and Lewis were the finalists between whom the judges had to decide. When the "gay virtuosity and flashing satire" of Lewis was preferred over "the ponderous and solemn" work of Dreiser, the naturalist, according to Lewis's biographer Mark Schorer "sulked in his tent."[3]

And even though by 1930 Dreiser had understandably become something of a stoic regarding his chances of ever receiving this ultimate recognition for his pioneering efforts in realism, the worldwide accolades showered upon the author of *Babbitt* and *Arrowsmith* hit hard.

Dreiser, the old "pro," seemed to be relegated to the sidelines while the fresh young buck was sent in to score the winning touchdown. The defeat was mitigated only by sporadic outcries from disappointed critics who thought that Dreiser of all living Americans should have been honored first and by Lewis's self-effacing remarks in praise of Dreiser in his acceptance speech in Stockholm. Lewis announced to the staid assemblage:

> I am sure you know by now that the award to me of the Nobel Prize was by no means altogether popular in America, doubtless an experience not altogether new to you.
>
> Suppose you had taken Theodore Dreiser. Now to me, as to many other American writers, Dreiser, more than any other man, is marching alone. Usually unappreciated, often hounded, he has cleared the trail from Victorian Howellsian timidity and gentility in American fiction to honesty, boldness, and passion of life. Without his pioneering I doubt if any of us could, unless we liked to be sent to jail, seek to express life, beauty and terror.[4]

Lewis could hardly have said more, and even this much was atypical of that acid-mouthed satirist. Nevertheless, while the words surely were balm to Dreiser's wound, they could not bring him the prize itself.[5]

On top of these disappointments came the premiere of the Famous Players' motion-picture production of *An American Tragedy.* Dreiser, the guest of honor, stalked out in a violent temper. He condemned the picture as being a complete travesty of his work, as disemboweling his novel of its basic themes and reducing his tragedy to a cops-and-robbers farce. Charging the movies with a "cheap commercialism" that led them into "toadying to the lowest and most insignificant tastes," he instituted a legal injunction against the film company to stop the picture from being shown, but his court action failed. Ironically, many present-day admirers of Dreiser's novel who have seen the Famous Players' version agree that the film violates Dreiser's themes considerably less than the author believed and that, in fact, it retains much of its power even after 60 years.

Chapter Seven

God and Mammon: *The Bulwark*

I need about 1,500 [words] to finish *The Bulwark* this winter.
— Dreiser, 1914

I am (I think) just one month off from finishing *The Bulwark*.
— Dreiser, 1945

Dreiser's chronicle of Solon Barnes, Quaker, was the last novel he completed during his lifetime and the one that took him the longest time, altogether, to finish. He conceived the idea sometime around 1910, soon after his friend Louise Campbell told him the story of her Quaker family — 36 years before its publication. He discussed the *Bulwark* project with Edgar Lee Masters in 1912; in 1914 he wrote H. L. Mencken that by September he intended making a stab at writing this "dandy story." He made more than a stab; a first draft was completed and sent in that year to Louise Campbell, by now serving as his typist-editor. But other affairs intervened, and the manuscript remained in Campbell's apartment till 1942. When she came across the bulky package in a storage closet, she wrote Dreiser apprising him of her discovery and coincidentally found him at work on a new and different version.[1]

All along he had wanted desperately to finish his last two volumes, this and *The Stoic*, both initiated so many years before. Failing in health, he rallied with Helen's aid to put forth one last tremendous effort. *The Stoic* would never be wholly completed, but *The Bulwark* was written and sent to Doubleday. After so long a lapse, who can say how closely it approximated the story for which the seed was first sown in 1910?

The Inner Light That Failed

That Theodore Dreiser should eventually write about the plight of
the Quakers, the Plain People, surrounded by a world where the
acquisitive instinct ran riot and men madly erected temples to
money, may seem odd to some. But ever since Dreiser's childhood
days he had felt an attraction to the Quaker ideal. He identified it
with memories of his dreamy mother, whose religion was not that far
from Quakerism. He recalled her meditating in shadowed corners of
rented homes in Warsaw and Evansville. He remembered her
dressed in the Spartan black bonnet and dress of the Mennonites, a
costume so simple it reminded him of male garb. Moreover her
nature was peaceful, and she was unobsessed with property or
wealth. Now and again in his stories Quaker references find a use,
but usually they furnish events with an ironic twist. For instance,
Carrie Meeber, clothes-crazy and mad for fame, achieves her first
stage triumph gowned as a modest Quaker. And Charles T. Yerkes,
for whom the profit motive is all, descended from a distinguished
line of orthodox Quaker progenitors (a fact that Dreiser knew but
omitted from *The Financier*).

Dreiser generally had little to say in his fiction that favored any
type of religion. Wherever possible he preferred to dismiss the whole
subject with a derisive phrase. When forced to address the issue by
events or by the white heat of an emotional tirade, he would pen
scathing pages lambasting the religionists: "Out upon them for a
swinish mass! Shut up the churches, knock down the steeples! Harry
them until they know the true place of religion – a weak man's
shield!"[2]

Yet Dreiser, perhaps paradoxically, did admire the Quaker
system and had read deeply in such basic documents as *The Book of
Discipline* and the *Journals* of Quaker leaders George Fox and John
Woolman.

So well versed was he in these and secondary volumes written
by outstanding Friends that in the 1930s he felt equipped to deliver
lectures before audiences in Quaker colleges. He even took under
consideration the reissuing of Woolman's *Journal*, prefaced by the
1871 introduction by John Greenleaf Whittier. This plan did not
materialize, but Dreiser did accept an invitation to edit *The Living
Thoughts of Thoreau*. The author of *Walden* appealed to him on

much the same basis of conspicuous idealism. He envisioned the Quakers as heroic figures. In the face of overwhelming odds, they possessed the fortitude to reject self-interest, the profit motive, and the status symbols of clothing, property, and wealth – all marks of the American system. In 1938 he wrote Rufus H. Jones, chairman of the American Friends Service Committee: "I am very much interested in the Quaker ideal. Like yourself I rather feel that it is the direct road to – not so much a world religion as a world appreciation of the force that provides us all with this amazing experience called life" (Elias 1959, 3:822).

The Quakers were utopians; but, the world being far too much with us, Dreiser could not help believing that Quakerism was doomed to strangulation by the octopus materialistic forces controlling society and men's passions. Thus *The Bulwark*, with all its compassion, inevitably became one of Dreiser's darkest stories. It is an American tragedy of another sort; it reads perhaps as Clyde's story would had it been written from the point of view of his missionary mother, Elvira Griffiths. Dreiser himself suggests this comparison with his great success, for he wrote Louise Campbell in 1945 that the manuscript, at last complete, was "about as long as *An American Tragedy* and about as tragic" (Campbell, 122). On the first count he was wrong – *The Bulwark* actually comes to a mere 337 pages, his shortest novel. But on the second count he was quite right.

Originally conceived at the time he was engrossed in *Jennie Gerhardt*, *The Bulwark* has more in common, as far as tone and feeling are concerned, with that study than with any of the other novels. The two belong side by side on his shelf. If Jennie is Dreiser's "pet heroine," then Solon Barnes is surely his pet hero – the only one, perhaps, that he thoroughly and genuinely admires. Both Jennie and Solon fail in life, but the compassion with which their failures are reported to us transcends pity.

Christian in Vanity Fair

Although *The Bulwark* is far less spectacular a work than *An American Tragedy*, a good case might be made for its more nearly approximating the idea of tragedy. Clyde Griffiths is tragic in the broadest conception only. To many readers he appears to be no more than a pitiful scrap of humanity, without stature of any sort.

But *The Bulwark* centers upon a protagonist who is considerably more capable of suggesting the stature of the classical tragic hero – a good man, a mature man who fails nevertheless in a lifelong struggle against the encroachments of worldly values.

Solon Barnes is so grounded in his religion that it comes to him instinctually; life without it is incomprehensible. He is epitomized by his author as "a good man – one of the nation's bulwarks."[3] If Solon is truly as worthy of being idealized as Dreiser describes him, then the nation is in a bad way; for the murky floods of materialism engulf Solon, more subtly, more gradually, perhaps, than they drown Clyde, but with no less certitude.

Solon's tragic flaw is an oversimplified view of life. At an early age he has divided the world arbitrarily into good and bad. In a universe guarded and governed by Divine Providence, the virtuous ultimately must be rewarded, he reasons. Likewise, the bad must be condemned. Quakerism constitutes Solon's firm foundation. By holding himself and his children steadfastly to its tenets, he originally conceives of his family's road to paradise as lying ready, broad, and clean-swept. But his own life passage provides him with two rather sobering lessons. He learns, for one thing, that life is far more complex than he has dreamed; good and bad are being mingled inseparably in every human affair. He also learns that, in America particularly, no man is an island but part of the continent and that he has no effective tools for walling out the pagan forces that infest the land.

In his introduction to the novel Dreiser defines the predicament in which Solon will act as protagonist. Quakerism, eulogized as the haven of idealism and perfection "in a none too perfect world," has striven to establish a tenable equilibrium between it and the disparate claims of the world, a coexistence, a balance "without flaw or shadow or error." Because this vision can be no more than a wonderful dream, the religion of George Fox, like so many other utopian visions, is destined to fall against the onslaught of the everyday world with its attractive vices, its chilling deprivations, its sad inequities, its "ordinary routine materiality."

But as long as Quakerism is allowed safely to isolate itself physically in America, the illusion of perfection can be maintained. Thus Rufus and Hannah Barnes, Solon's parents, face no real challenge so long as they remain on their isolated acres in a remote corner of nineteenth-century Maine, northernmost of the states and a place at that time relatively untouched by the main current of American industrial-urban society. But upon the death of Hannah's brother-in-law, the family inherits his property and moves to southern New Jersey. Although their new home stands in a community of Friends, it is a community too intimately mingled with things non-Quaker to remain untainted by the money ideal. Even Phoebe Kimber, a relative and as dedicated a Quaker as one might hope to find, proposes the geographical move to Rufus on the basis of the prosperity of the Philadelphia area and the "advantages" that nearby schools offer over those of Maine.

What Solon must learn, but can learn only to his sorrow, is simply this: the world is so corrosive a despoiler that no compromise between materialism and idealism is possible. For Quakers, coexistence with the way society has organized itself is a delusion. Hide as one might, the insidious triumph of materialism will be inevitable.

In *The Bulwark* this conflict is symbolized first by the family's residence at Thornbrough, a pretentious antebellum mansion now owned by Phoebe. Even in disrepair, the house retains "an echo of ease and comfort . . . a kind of social grandeur" such as the Barnes family has never experienced. Surrounded by its ornate iron fence, the Thornbrough property is cut by curving driveways leading to carved oak doors, inside of which Rufus for the first time comes "face to face with the form, if not actually the present substance, of luxury." An elaborate reception hall forested with pillars, clearly intended for glittering social gatherings; crystal-prismed chandeliers designed to make jewels and silks gleam; a handsome staircase of carved and polished walnut down which impressive entrances may be possible – every detail of the house implies not only waste and show but "greed, drunkenness, immorality, and the other sins of living which George Fox and the faith he proclaimed had so valiantly sought to put aside forever."

The house at Thornbrough, in short, is no place for solid, staid Quakers. Rufus stands before it open-mouthed, timorous as a skater who has already tied on his blades when he spies the DANGER – THIN ICE sign on the river. The only proper action – and Rufus's first impulse – is to retreat. He should sell the house as soon as possible to some poor soul who sets store by display. It is the only way to sidestep this devilish temptation.

But the house is not Rufus's to sell. It belongs to Phoebe Kimber, and she has invited him to live in it – only temporarily, of course. He will repair, paint, landscape, and make the property marketable, for it cannot be disposed of advantageously until it has been rendered suitable for use as a country home. Then some wealthy Philadelphian out to make a social splash will buy it. In this manner Rufus makes his first hazardous compromise with materialism. The needed restorations involve a state of luxurious living that he recognizes as being totally incompatible with his religious beliefs; yet, as steward of the widowed Phoebe's property, he feels obligated to render the house salable: "Between the two horns of this dilemma – simplicity for himself and reasonable luxury for a possible buyer – he was fairly caught" (*Bulwark*, 12).

Rufus attempts to save himself by way of another compromise: restoring the house in as simple a manner as he can manage and then living in as small and unpretentious a portion of it as possible. But what seems a solution is actually his first disastrous step into quicksand, for Phoebe in gratitude refuses to deed her restored house to anyone but Rufus or his children. Rufus considers this proposal. His family is comfortably established, and the Barneses appear to be surviving without apparent detriment to their Quakerism. Rufus concludes it is far easier to remain at Thornbrough than to risk offending the generous Phoebe. This first concession made, others will follow. And then still others. While Rufus himself strays no farther than a step toward toleration of things non-Quaker – and the same might be said, though with less conviction, for his son Solon – the family's wholesale embracing of worldly values awaits only the passage of time.

God's Gold

Rufus Barnes's son Solon comes to live at Thornbrough at the age of ten. Solidly under his parents' influence, he at first is not visibly infected by the luxury of the estate. Yet, growing up accustomed to the spaciousness, the fine woodwork, and the craftsmanship that everywhere delights the senses, Solon lacks the full recognition of the disparity, which had so disturbed his father, between this house and his religious tenets. Are not the walls of the home covered with homely Quaker mottos and truisms? Has not the Barnes family life remained plain, even amid this grandeur?

Solon's first awakening to "the problem of wealth as opposed to simplicity" comes with his youthful attachment to Benecia Wallin, later his wife. Benecia's father, Justus Wallin, has been shrewd in his stewardship of the properties Providence has granted him. Consequently, he has become an even more worldly and prosperous Quaker than Rufus Barnes. He is quick to note signs of affection between Solon and Benecia. Impressed with Solon's business acumen, Wallin invites the Barnes family to his grand home on Philadelphia's Girard Avenue. The visit is a revelation to Solon: "There were carved mahogany tables and chairs, parqueted floors strewn with rugs and animal skins, and large ornate vases filled with flowers and grasses. Soon after they entered the living room a servant appeared, offering silver plates containing tall glasses of fruit juice – a procedure which astonished and somewhat disconcerted the entire Barnes family" (*Bulwark*, 51). Here Solon gains his first insight into the drastic encroachments of the materialistic spirit upon the Quaker community. More revelations follow.

He becomes aware of disturbing numbers of Quakers who compromise their ideals or abandon them altogether to the claims of wealth and display. He notes his cousin, Rhoda Kimber, sprung from the same stock as he, yet "consciously out to go somewhere in this world, and not . . . at all interested in the Quaker idea of plainness." Rhoda falls away from Quakerism through marriage, becoming rich and socially prominent. Rhoda is of an age with Solon, but in her family the acids of materialism have had an extra generation during which to etch their evils. Were Solon sufficiently perceptive, he might foresee the troubles that lie ahead for his own children.

But Solon, unfortunately, is a poor judge of people. In the black-and-white world he constructs for himself, he continually misreads others. His thinking is dangerously simplistic. Expecting that all Quakers will be good people, he presumes that they are. The rest of the world's inhabitants, while they may chance to be good, are very likely evil. "He did not know life. Rather, to him, all those who had sinned were thoroughly bad, their souls irredeemable" (*Bulwark*, 6)

As a young clerk in the Traders and Builders Bank, Solon witnesses a street scuffle. Intervening, he apprehends the victim while the thief makes off with the stolen wallet. This duplicity of

appearances, superimposed on his simple view of life, is deranging to
Solon. At the bank a young boy, Walter Briscoe, is trusted by Solon
principally because he is a Quaker. But the boy embezzles money.
Discovery of the theft shakes Solon "to the very core of his moral
being." When the Quaker father begs another chance for his son,
Solon refuses; but Walter is no sooner sentenced to the penitentiary
than Solon recognizes his moral error. Recalling his Quaker *Book of
Discipline* – "If a man be overtaken in a fault, ye which are spiritual,
restore such an one in the spirit of meekness, convincing thyself, lest
thee also be tempted" (*Bulwark*, 119-20) – Solon acknowledges his
own serious offense against his religious principles.

Troubling as such episodes prove, Solon remains convinced that
his feet tread the path of righteousness. Active participation in the
financial world might be expected to dismay even the most steadfast
of Quakers, but so blindly confident in his faith is Solon that to take
on the life of a banker gives him little direct anguish. He strides
rapidly toward wealth, a condition of life that his youth at Thornbrough has well prepared him to rationalize. "We surely have been
favored by Providence; that is, if it intends that we should enjoy or
display so many luxuries," he remarks to Benecia after they are
settled in the new home presented to them by Justus (*Bulwark*,
103). The place is furnished lavishly – and most un-Quakerlike –
with Sheraton, Chippendale, and Hepplewhite furniture, fine linens
and crystal, and a small fortune in silver, china, brass, and copper-
ware. With his marriage settlement of $40,000 and with an auspicious
career under way at the Traders and Builders, Solon realizes "the
dream of his schooldays come true: a good position, a handsome
home, a beautiful young wife, powerful friends and relatives, health
and strength" (*Bulwark*, 104).

It is all much too good to be true. "A lust for wealth and power
[is] in the air," yet Solon feels he has managed to keep his own
hands clean. Desirous of success, but not at the expense of his principles, he avoids monopolistic dealings, preferring instead "simpler
realms where profits were comparatively small and the troubled face
of ethics was not so plainly visible" (*Bulwark*, 104). Under the
philosophy that a beneficent God holds His beloved earth in the
palm of His hand and is in supreme control, Solon sees "everything
in terms of divine order." No matter how darkly they might be
obscured, he believes that all events run according to divine will,

toward an ultimate good. Any concentration of wealth, therefore, also must be part of the divine pattern. And there is always the precious *Book of Discipline* to guide the individual: "When any become possessed of ample means, they should remember that they are duly stewards who must render an account for the right use of the things committed to their care" (*Bulwark*, 38). Hence, Solon's wealth is a sacred trust for him to guard and guide.

One day an old man, desperate for cash, sells Solon his chicken farm at a fraction of its market value. Is this right? It is good business, surely, but how fully is it in accord with Quaker dictates of justice? Solon ponders this question. On another occasion he purchases at public auction a block of houses for $17,000. He already has in mind a prospective buyer who will take the houses for $27,000, exactly the type of transaction to spur an ordinary young man to even more profitable manipulations. But the deal troubles Solon. Where is the dividing line between right and wrong? How does one determine in any given case the fine border between good stewardship and greed, "between the desire for power and wealth and a due regard for Quaker precepts?" (*Bulwark*, 113).

Solon's business associates give him even more pause. The Traders and Builders Bank is a staid concern at first, conservative and ethical. But as time passes, new directors enter. Who are they? One is Skidmore, a Quaker and director of the bank, yet possessed of "a most pretentious house in Rittenhouse Square." Others are Wilkerson, Seay, Baker, "exactly of the temperament which organizes, suborns, controls." These are men devoid of morals in financial matters. Discovering that his fellow directors are taking advantage of a law allowing banks to invest depositors' funds and then investing these funds in shaky concerns controlled by themselves, Solon is deeply grieved.

Affairs soon have drifted beyond his power to rationalize or excuse. A clean break with the bank seems the only honorable solution. He resigns his position. Financially, Solon is little affected, being well along in years by now and solidly taken care of. What is important is his implicit admission that the economic system dominating Philadelphia – and the nation – cannot be bucked by men like himself; it can only be seceded from. If his public career is ended, his religious principles appear to have survived.

"In Much Love to the Rising Generation"

Had Solon remained childless, it might have been relatively simple
for him to strike a balance between the material and the ideal. As it
is, Dreiser employs the world's corruption of the rising generation to
demonstrate the craftiness with which the worm has bored its way to
the apple's heart. Solon and Benecia produce five offspring. From
their tenderest years Solon hopes to inculcate these five with the
spirit of his own vigorous Quakerism. He determines to provide a
perfect home atmosphere, one which will protect his children
against the corrosive influences that have touched his own life but
have not, he persists in believing, tainted it. Growing up in such an
environment, how could the new generation help but blossom into
"perfect examples of well-brought-up children: earnest, truthful, just
and kind"?

Isobel, Orville, Dorothea, Etta, Stewart: one by one Solon
Barnes's children are born – and one by one they bewilder Solon as
their disparate natures confound his well-meant plans for their
futures. The oversimplified world he has created in order to accom-
modate his theories begins to crumble even before the children are
out of their cradles. It is Solon's great sorrow to watch the emerging
personalities take their own directions, irrespective of his surveil-
lance. As the twig is bent so grows the tree – this is his axiom. Yet
his children persist in following paths not of his choosing but of
nature's. "They are born so."

His daughter Isobel, born without physical attractiveness but
with a highly sensitive and perceptive nature, early realizes the
"sharp distinction" between herself and the pretty girls at school. By
degrees she is backed into a shell of introspection. She is passive,
lacking the mysterious magnetism that can spark friendship or love.
Aware of the trap of spinsterhood, she yearns for marriage. But no
suitors appear, and her own timidity prevents her from seeking them
out. She drifts into unhappy loneliness.

Isobel's sisters are equally singular. Dorothea, beautiful and
sensual by inclination, spends her youth "dreaming of her eventual
escape from quiet Thornbrough" and into the world of society with
its display of jewels and gowns. In contrast, Etta, the youngest of the
girls, is born dreamy and romantic, of an artistic bent. Etta exists in a
world of her own ideals. She is the type of girl who, chancing to see

a young couple kissing, thinks *this is love;* who, reading *La Dame aux Camelias,* feels a new world of "romance and reality" opening for her.

The natures of Solon's two sons are no less different. Orville is a born conservative, "a saver of pennies" destined to worship the idol of reputation. Stewart from his earliest years is "a veritable fire-brand" in pursuit of pleasure. As the boys mature, their natures only assert themselves more forcefully. Orville is drawn to the wealthier Quaker relatives, whose handsome homes, servants, gardens, horses and carriages he admires. Stewart takes his material ease for granted and is attracted by the powerful excitements of "color, motion, beauty, the more vivid forms of life." He is a born rebel, dominated by sensuality, preoccupied with sex.

Five children, sprung from the same parents, nurtured in the same Edenic environment, yet what separate paths they take! The true substance and import of *The Bulwark* lies in the tracing of their careers from birth. Without these stories Dreiser's novel would contain no more than a pale and relatively pointless shadow of his philosophy. But through the children and their various experiences, Dreiser tells us two things of consequence. First, the dominant influences on a human being are the inborn "chemisms" that combine with whatever social and economic forces rule society to produce the eventual adult. Second, the influence of home environment is a comparatively trivial one. If *An American Tragedy* left any residual implication that a different, less restricted childhood might have altered Clyde Griffiths, events in *The Bulwark* pretty well demolish the theory. Clyde would have been Clyde irrespective of his rearing, just as Solon Barnes's children become more and more distinguishably themselves as the years pass. The influence of home environment diminishes considerably in the face of societal pressures. Here Dreiser's naturalism asserts itself strongly, diminishing the power of the individual and placing an emphasis upon the large, somewhat inchoate forces that rule life in the end.

"Life Was Very Strange"

As his children emerge into young adulthood Solon is confronted with an insuperable problem. Faced by the enigma of life, he comes to recognize his error: he has oversimplified the world's organizing principles. This realization bewilders him. How mistaken to imagine that his children would be carbon copies of himself, instilled with his own principles and strong enough, with the guidance of a religious home training, to find their satisfactory balance between God and Mammon! "Solon did not quite realize that while he might be able thus to control their outward conduct, it was not possible to control the minds of his children" (*Bulwark*, 168-69). Orville, whom Solon considers most like himself and therefore most successful, is in reality an insufferable snob. Orville looks like Solon, acts like Solon, succeeds even more brilliantly than Solon, but he possesses no more substance than a meringue. His religion is a mere badge of respectable conformity. He marries a wealthy girl, Althea Stoddard, to whom the precepts of Quakerism are important not in any religious sense but socially. "But with such a marriage he would be rich, secure, comfortable, respected, and admired, and he wanted no more than that in this world" (*Bulwark*, 149). Dorothea and Orville become very close, and rightly so, for they are stamped from the same die. With the help of her Aunt Rhoda, Dorothea marries the son of a street-railway magnate in a ceremony designed for maximum social impact. The guest lists for the wedding are checked against the Social Register. Orville and Dorothea are lost irrevocably to Mammon, but Solon is unable to discern it.

What Solon is able to see is the manner in which his other children fall short of Orville's and Dorothea's achievements. Matriculated at Llewellyn College, Isobel finds life miserable, since the college provides only the most watered-down remnants of true Quaker atmosphere. It has dwindled into little more than a factory for transforming commonplace girls into snobs. The more that the social cliques on campus exclude her, the more Isobel retreats to her dormitory room and her studies; she is convinced that there is "nothing in store for one so poorly equipped physically as she."

Unable to help Isobel in her despair, Solon questions the meaning, purpose, and direction of life. Heretofore, he has believed all things to be ruled by Divine Providence and contrived for the ultimate good of earth's children. Now, in order to retain his faith, he must believe in the possibility that some hidden blessing is intended in Isobel's tragedy. What that may be escapes him. Clearly, he must help the girl develop what charms and abilities she has been granted. But how? And to what end? Hold as Solon will to his Quaker

tenets, the seeds of doubt are sown: "It was another of those illuminating truths about life which Solon was being compelled to learn,
but very slowly, namely, that in spite of a divinely ordered scheme of
things and a willingness on the part of anyone to ally himself with the
manifested plan, as far as one could determine it, still these things
would occur" (*Bulwark*, 127).

Isobel remains a worry to her father, but since she is an
outwardly placid, quiet, dutiful girl, she provokes no family crisis;
instead she silently succumbs to her own misery.

It takes Isobel's younger siblings, Etta and Stewart, to smash
through the respectable facade by which Solon has set so much
store. They create problems affecting their father with more immedi-
acy. Etta is allowed to enter Oakwold College, where she comes
under the influence of Volida La Porte, a thorough "modern" who
introduces the girl to disreputable literature in books such as
Daudet's *Sappho* and leads her toward what in her thinking constitute new horizons of intellectual and artistic discovery. Solon,
asserting his paternalistic authority, gives Etta an ultimatum to abandon Volida. In rebellious response, she pawns her mother's jewels to
obtain the funds necessary to leave Philadelphia and join her friend
at the University of Wisconsin. She has made her break and will not
return home. The two girls eventually travel to New York. Etta, now
converted to a new order and lost to Quakerism, becomes the
mistress of a Greenwich Village artist. Orville, stumbling on knowledge of the affair, panics for selfish fear of some public notoriety that
might damage his own social reputation. He demands that the relationship cease at once. Etta refuses, recognizing that "the hateful
reproaches of Orville emanated from a small mind, full of greed and
ambition for worldly success, and she was glad that she was no
longer a part of such a world." Significantly, Solon, when dealing
with a transgressor, at least remained conscious of Quaker teachings;
but Orville gives no thought whatsoever to helping Etta find her way
back to her former principles. From now on, she is no sister of his.

Etta causes a minimum of distress to her parents. Redemption of
the jewels enables Solon to hide the theft from Benecia, and the
other children contrive to keep Solon unapprised of Etta's love
affair. But in Stewart's case notoriety is not so easily quashed; it
provides the dynamite that will blast Solon's crumbling world.

Stewart's sensual nature drives him into companionship with rich college friends, devotees of fast cars and girls; and when, for financial reasons, he finds himself unable to keep pace with his cohorts, he looks for ways and means of obtaining money. One immediate resource is his Aunt Rhoda, who determines to cultivate her good-looking nephew as she had his sister Dorothea. Thus, ironically, one Quaker corrupts another. But even Rhoda's generosity has a limit, and Stewart steals, first with timidity, then brazenly, from his mother's purse, from Orville's wallet, from his roommate's desk.

Stewart's dissolute life, tame as it has been until now, flares into catastrophe on a wild automobile ride. One of the boys, determined to overcome his girl's scruples, slips into her drink a nerve remedy pilfered from his mother's medicine chest. Ordinarily these drops, which are a sort of tranquilizer, produce no more than a mood of assent. But, unbeknown to the boys, the girl has a heart weakness that is fatally aggravated by the drops. Instead of securing a physician, the panicky youths dump her by a lonely roadside. At dawn she is found dead; and the boys, having made it "practically impossible for the police not to track them down," are soon behind bars.

Now the winds of scandal are loosed, and there is no escape for the family. Stewart commits suicide in jail. Benecia, who has been so protected from any inkling of family trouble that she is incapable of enduring this shock, dies of heartbreak. Solon is dazed. What has so dimmed the inner light that was to cast such radiance on all their lives? "Had he not done all in his power to obviate any such deadly consequence in connection with his family?" How and where had his stewardship gone so awry?

The Mare of the World

When Solon was a child, his mother had been terrorized by a dream concerning him. She saw her son leap astride a handsome black mare, stoutly thwarting the animal's attempts to throw him off. The mare had snorted and pawed the earth, reared on its hind legs, swung to left and right, but had been incapable of unseating its rider. Then, when it most appeared Solon might break the mare to his will, the horse had rushed a fence, torn the rider from his seat, and thrown him. At the sight of her son unconscious on the ground,

Hannah Barnes awoke, cold with perspiration at the possible significance of the dream:

> That beautiful mare, its friendly actions and then its subsequent erratic,
> murderous conduct. And Solon, all the while, up to the moment he was in the
> saddle, seemingly so confident of the mare's friendly and obedient spirit.
>   What could it mean? . . . there was the feeling that in some way or other it
> might be connected with . . . the sudden shift in their material and social
> status. (*Bulwark*, 61-62)

And so it is. The dream foreshadows Solon's struggle to tame the
materialistic forces rampant in the world, to subordinate them and
sensuality to the religious will. But instead the mare of the world at
last throws him, and disastrously.

"I Am Crying for Life"

In the closing chapters of *The Bulwark*, Solon Barnes meditates on
the fate of his house, stricken like Job's for reasons he cannot
fathom. Then by slow degrees, he finds his faith in God revitalized by
a rediscovery of the beneficence of the creative force that lies behind
all life, even its tragedies, and by recourse to the *Journal* of John
Woolman. Here it becomes rather apparent that Dreiser, with his last
book, is offering a final, rather drastically revised estimate of his own
father.

In his autobiography he had described John Paul Dreiser as
"wandering distrait and forlorn amid a storm of difficulties: age, the
death of his wife, the flight of his children, doubt as to their salvation, poverty, a declining health."[4] This same catalog (barring
poverty, of course) accurately depicts Solon Barnes in his last days.
Both men are strongly religious fathers who attempt to raise their
families according to the codes they have accepted for themselves.
Both see their sons and daughters seduced into a world which to
them, because it is irreligious, can only be evil. The Barnes children,
like the young Dreisers, "could not help being confronted by the
marked contrast between the spirit of the . . . home and that of the
world at large. In spite of the many admirable qualities of the home,
these were distinctly at variance with the rush and swing and spirit of
the time itself, and this fact could scarcely fail to impress even the

least impressionable minds" (*Bulwark*, 138). Supposing Theodore
Dreiser intended the character of Solon Barnes to stand as a portrait
of the elder Dreiser, then Theodore's often reiterated antipathy for
his father and his church must somehow be squared with this
compassionate portrayal of the Quaker. The answer lies in time, with
its merciful tendency to leach the bitterness from early memories.
The novelist, says Helen Dreiser, after his father's death "recalled
traits in him, too, that he admired: his honesty, his austere Germanic
way of living – and there grew in his mind the desire to build a story
around him" (H. Dreiser, 290).

Dreiser's long and bitter antagonism toward Catholicism had not
really waned very much, even though as he aged he grew less caustic
in his expressed attitude toward religion generally. Now, in the
interests of objectivity, he was able to alter the religion of his protagonist from Catholic to Quaker. Some memories had cut too deeply to
deal with, perhaps, and he seemed to wish that his last novel should
point toward praise, not indictment. He finally was prepared to
forgive. Life was life, after all. He had always insisted that in life there
was no black and no white; there were only victims. Why, then,
should he search for scapegoats?

Dreiser had pointed toward such a positive portrait of his father
for many years. It may be true that his extremely long delay in
completing *The Bulwark* can be attributed to the psychological
block against portraying his father in bright light. Only time could
shift that block, but even a hasty survey of his fiction reveals a steady,
if glacially slow, softening of hostile lines, as bit by bit his own maturity, combined with his accumulated observation of life, aided him to
put aside old quarrels. Dreiser's autobiographies are marked initially
by attacks on his father that can only be termed savage – venomous
portraits, really. They modify very slowly. First there is only the most
grudging admission that there may be more than one side to his
father. Then comes pity, then understanding, and ultimately sympathy. By 1940 Dreiser could declare by letter that his father had been
"a truthful man and a devout Catholic" (Elias 1959, 3:887). But he
still insisted that "if I have a battle cry, it is this: Destroy the Catholic
Church in every land on the face of the earth" (Elias 1959, 3:705). To
distinguish the father from the institution was essential.

Such a pattern had been inaugurated long ago. In *Jennie
Gerhardt*, which contains Dreiser's first sympathetic portrait of his

father, Lutheranism was rather consciously substituted for Catholicism. Edward Butler in *The Financier* reminds one of John Dreiser, but Butler remains a Catholic and the portrait is not flattering. The father in *The Hand of the Potter* becomes Jewish and is compassionately drawn. The most ingenious solution to the parentage dilemma occurs in *An American Tragedy*. Dreiser's inclination, when relying upon his family for source material, was to follow the archetype composed of the ineffectual but stringently religious father and the pliant, admirable mother who follows the father's lead. In the *Tragedy* this pattern is altered sufficiently to combine both parents in one. Elvira Griffiths possesses not only the commendable traits of Dreiser's mother, but also the religious drive of the father; as a result, Asa Griffiths hovers in the background, something of a ghost, not really essential to the story.

When at last Dreiser felt psychologically prepared to focus upon the father *as* father, the solution evident in *The Bulwark* appears to have suggested itself to him. The solution was a long time dawning and the novel was completed only in the nick of time. Dreiser returned his galley proofs of *The Bulwark* to Doubleday at the end of August 1945, hoping to make them ready for publication in February or March 1946. On 28 December, after suffering an acute kidney attack, he died.

Dreiser, this "foggy giant" who solitarily from his tragic peak viewed life as confused, unjust, and without light for earthlings, left no children. But had he been survived, his sons and daughters might easily have echoed the words Dreiser himself gave to Etta Barnes as she emerged from the funeral service for her father: "Oh, I am not crying for myself, or for Father – I am crying for *life.*"

Chapter Eight

Dreiser Studies:
The First Half-Century

Dreiser is a dull, pompous, dated, and darned near ridiculous writer.
>   – Dorothy Parker, 1931

He is a high water-mark.
>   – Dorothy Dudley, 1932

The first edition of this book concluded with a spirited defense of
Dreiser as a writer. During the early years of his career, his method,
especially in matters of literary style, had come under bitter attack.
He was said to be blundering, awkward, confused in his diction,
lacking in taste, and, at times, not even a writer at all. Even in his
years of fame praise all too often came grudgingly, and he was likely
to be dubbed "the world's worst great writer." Today that attitude
has changed considerably, and this chapter will document the
continuing controversy that eventually led to that change. It is not
that Dreiser has been discovered, belatedly, to be a graceful stylist.
His weaknesses remain for all the world to see. But we perceive
more clearly now that the man should be judged less for his manner
than for his matter. He had something important and basic to say
about life, especially about life in America, and he said it in novels
and stories that retain an amazing portion of their original power. At
his best, he still is a gripping, sometimes a breathtaking narrator.

Dreiser's Reputation: 1900-1910

From the beginning, Dreiser proved to be a controversial figure.
Even before the actual publication of *Sister Carrie*, he was engaged
in a heated battle with his publisher, Doubleday, who wished to
cancel his contract and withdraw the novel from its list of forthcom-

ing books, actions Dreiser successfully opposed. The victory proved
to be a Pyrrhic one, however, when Doubleday failed adequately to
push the novel in the marketplace. Reviewers wavered between
praise and condemnation, a type of reception to which Dreiser
would become accustomed. His novel was described as "too realistic, too sombre" "unhealthful in tone," and "a most unpleasant tale
[which] you would never dream of recommending to another person
to read."[1] On the other hand, it was described elsewhere as strong
and fearless, painting "a picture of startling intensity," as "one of the
most powerful [novels] of the past year in all respects," and as "a
remarkable book, strong, virile, written with the clear determination
of a man who has a story to tell and who tells it" (Salzman, 1, 6, 9).
Reviews following the publication of *Sister Carrie* in England in 1901
were considerably more encouraging, and the critical reception of
the novel upon its American republication in 1907 brought further
praise for its truth and frankness, one reviewer calling it "the
strongest piece of realism we have yet met with in American fiction."
But the same reviewer felt obliged to warn that *Sister Carrie* would
remind many readers of a novel such as Emile Zola's *Nana*, which at
that time was generally considered to be notorious, a salacious
picture of degraded life in France. To counteract this, the reviewer
defended Dreiser's treatment of a similar theme as "clean and
unpornographic" (Salzman, 44).

Among the reactions to *Sister Carrie* were any number of
derogatory comments concerning Dreiser's method of handling the
language, which was awkward in more instances than a novelist
might like to have called to his attention, stilted and high-flown in
one passage, excessively slangy in another, in all quite different from
the typically formal prose expected in a popular novel at the turn of
the century. At least one reviewer described the book as suffering
from an "utter lack of any approach to a literary manner of diction,"
pointing out "inelegancies (not to say vulgarities)" such as the
constructions "swashed around with a great air," "he was crazy to
have Carrie alone," and "he wondered how he would get ahead of
the drummer" (Salzman, 16). That sentences such as these produce
no shock in the contemporary reader is one indication of the
distance American prose has traveled in its passage toward informal-
ity. The battle for the use of the vernacular was just beginning.
Dreiser played a considerable – and pioneering – role in winning it.

Deepening Controversy: 1910-1920

The critical battle over Dreiser's books took a turn for the worse after 1912, further polarizing those forces that praised the novelist rather uncritically and those that slapped him down with outright rejection.

That the image of Dreiser as a literary immoralist had been established as an accepted fact is made evident by what may be the first accounts of his novels in a reference book. Ernest A. Baker's *A Guide to the Best Fiction in English* (1913) cites the two Dreiser novels published at the time of compilation, *Sister Carrie* and *Jennie Gerhardt*. Of the first, Baker argues that its "chief interest" is the "exhaustive record of the career of a young woman led into vice, and the careful study of a man's moral deterioration."[2] Baker's almost exclusive concentration on deviations from accepted proprieties is continued in his description of Jennie as the victim of "the pleasure-loving son of the enterprising Irishman, who illustrates the vices and dangers of our complicated and materialized social organization." Dreiser's new novels fared no better; in fact, their reception affirmed and even intensified the controversy over his fiction. *The Financier* (1912) brought an avalanche of praise mixed with condemnation, *The Titan* (1914) more of the same, and *The "Genius"* (1915), under attack by the New York Society for the Suppression of Vice, was withdrawn from the marketplace by its publisher. It remained effectively banned until 1923.

The controversy awaited only powerful voices that would bring the issue to a head. One such voice belonged to the prominent midwestern critic Stuart P. Sherman, whose essay, "The Barbaric Naturalism of Mr. Dreiser," appeared in the *Nation* in 1915. In an outright and vociferous condemnation, Sherman attacked Dreiser's adherence to the naturalistic theories propounded by Zola and derived essentially from Charles Darwin's *The Origin of Species* (1859). To write from such a viewpoint on life was to reduce human existence to the level of animal life, which in Sherman's view was a wholly unacceptable stance. "Mr. Dreiser drives home the great truth," declared Sherman in his ironic tone, "that man is essentially an animal, impelled by temperament, instinct, physics, chemistry – anything you please that is irrational and uncontrollable. . . . Mr. Dreiser reduces the problem of the novelist to the lowest possible

terms [by espousing a philosophy that] quite excludes him from the
field in which a great realist must work." Replete with specific references to the five novels Dreiser had published by 1915, Sherman
labeled all of Dreiser's fiction as lying "curiously outside American
society" as that society was generally seen by clear-eyed observers,
and he closed his essay with a syllogism hammering home that same
"truth": "A naturalistic novel is a representation based upon a
theory of animal behavior. Since a theory of animal behavior can
never be an adequate basis for a representation of the life of man in
contemporary society, such a representation is an artistic blunder.
When half the world attempts to assert such a theory, the other half
rises in battle. And so one turns with relief from Mr. Dreiser's novels
to the morning papers" (Sherman, 80).

The "other half" to rise to the battle turned out to be H. L.
Mencken, Dreiser's new friend and a powerful critic in his own right,
a voice that became even more dominant throughout the 1920s. In
the period immediately following Sherman's denunciation, the
general American reader of novels, largely because of the notoriety
in the press surrounding The "Genius" case, was in a position to
paraphrase Emily Dickinson's remark concerning Walt Whitman:
"You speak of [Mr. Dreiser] – I never read his Book – but was told
that he was disgraceful . . . " To this attitude Mencken offered a
corrective in "The Dreiser Bugaboo," printed in Seven Arts in 1917.[3]
Reminding his readers that the great Mark Twain had recently been
declared as lacking any high artistic or moral aim, Mencken
dismissed Sherman's accusations as mere "irate flubdub" and "calm,
superior numskullery" more proper to the Victorian era than to the
enlightened twentieth century.

The Dreiser approach to life, insisted Mencken, had a long and
glorious history stretching back to the golden era of Greek literature.
Mencken's essay became a rejoinder to the censors who had succeeded in removing The "Genius" from bookstores, as well as a
frontal attack on "professorial smugness." By deliberately quoting
the specific passages in the novel that had been objected to, he did
his best to indicate that Dreiser's story and language were neither
obscene nor profane. What was really troubling Sherman, he
believed, was not any artistic shortcoming on Dreiser's part but
rather his failure to hew to the comfortable, established Christian
and American strictures regarding what was proper or improper in

fiction. Mencken argued that the deviations of pre-Dreiserian realistic writers from outdated orthodoxy were praiseworthy: "All the rubber-stamp formulae of American fiction were thrown overboard in these earlier books; instead of reducing the inexplicable to the obvious, they lifted the obvious to the inexplicable; one could find in them no orderly chain of causes and effects, of rewards and punishments; they represented life as a phenomenon at once terrible and unintelligible, like a stroke of lightning" (Mencken, 91).

Mencken saw Dreiser as being the latest and the most accomplished representative of the realistic tradition, a man whose work was not to be censured but read and appreciated. Mencken had been preceded by Randolph Bourne, writing in the *Dial* in 1916 and saying that Dreiser surpassed all other writers in picturing lower middle-class life in America because he approached his subject without crippling self-consciousness. He had managed to humanize the sex theme – always a primary target for the censors – and in *Sister Carrie* had achieved "a spontaneous working-out of mediocre, and yet elemental and significant, lives."[4] The things that Dreiser emphasized were those that characterized the "new America" that was struggling to become articulate, and in becoming the spokesman for that emerging world Dreiser necessarily had to flout the traditional American beliefs in optimism and redemption. Bourne, had he not died at an early age, might well have become the most significant champion of Dreiser and his books in the decade ahead.

Recognition: 1920-1930

Many of the early attacks on Dreiser's ability to write the English language – which swelled to a crescendo during the years between 1910 and 1917, receding only slightly during the decade of the 1920s – can now be seen as oblique and disguised attempts to jettison the Dreiser books on the basis of their unpopular moral or philosophical views. Of these two, the general understanding of his philosophical principles came about later, while his challenge to accepted standards of morality seemed to be more immediately understood and more easily disposed of. It was easy, for example, to complain that a novel such as *Sister Carrie* contained not a single "lady" or "gentleman" (as those terms were understood in the genteel tradition) or that in *The "Genius"* his interest lay merely in printing 763 pages concerned with "ungoverned sexual passion." To allow a loose woman such as Carrie to prosper was to flout the Victorian code that decreed that promiscuity must be punished – by death preferably, or at least by a penalty such as disease or ostracism. Novels such as *The Financier* and, even more so, *The Titan* attacked the established worship of wealth that was a chief manifestation of the industrial era; they inveighed against the laissez-faire economic policies that fostered the growth of the great fortunes and the political practices that were its bulwark. This aspect of Dreiser's work was not so readily comprehended, but his economic novels still invoked a sense of uneasiness sufficient to make him seem subversive to everything held dear by the generation in power between 1880 and World War I.

On the other side stood those defenders who shouted (when and where they were permitted to get into print), "Dreiser speaks truth!" But they were not always clear, either in their own minds or in their expression, as to precisely what important Truth was being spoken. Despite the publication of such pioneering works as Thorstein Veblen's *The Theory of the Leisure Class* (1899), one of the first major sociological works methodically to anatomize the American social system produced by the industrial era, the nation as a whole had not reached that degree of introspection that might clarify precisely what it was that Dreiser was attacking, or defending, as the case might be.

This was true even though Dreiser, in his autobiographical *A Book about Myself* (1922), was rather explicit in stating that his argument was with the enormous discrepancies produced by Social Darwinism, wherein the laws of nature, especially the concept of evolution, were held to be not only immutable but also operative on the human populace just as they were on the world of plants and animals. Nature knew best – that was the accepted principle. Nature must be left alone to work its magic in its own way. If untampered with by human meddlers, in good time nature would produce any necessary changes and solve all knotty problems in the manner most appropriate and beneficial. Hence the hands-off policy of laissez-faire government and the supremacy of "rugged individualism," the practice under which individuals were to be left free to battle for economic survival as determined by their fitness to rise or fall. In Dreiser's novels this policy had been dramatized in the abject failure of George Hurstwood, for which society accepted no responsibility and offered to help, as well as the triumph of Frank Cowperwood, who through amoral self-interest amassed millions.

What was not generally understood was that Dreiser saw the Capitalistic system itself as the great enemy. He attacked the very basis of the American way, for through its endorsement of monopolistic practices it made possible, even encouraged, the piling up of untold wealth and power in the hands of the "beautiful strong," as Dreiser's contemporary Stephen Crane had dubbed them in his poem "The Trees in the Garden Rained Flowers." On the other hand, large sections of the population knew unprecedented deprivation as a result of these same practices. In *A Book about Myself*, Dreiser wrote much about his observations of American economic practices during the 1880s and 1890s. In retrospect, he could see clearly that "America was just entering upon the most lurid phase of that vast, splendid, most lawless and most savage period in which the great financiers were plotting and conniving at the enslavement of the people." In his indictment, he named John D. Rockefeller, Andrew Carnegie, William H. Vanderbilt, Jay Gould, and others in a list that could well have included Charles T. Yerkes, whose buccaneering career he had fictionalized in *The Financier* and *The Titan.*

On every side, during his travels in the 1890s, Dreiser had become witness to the "vast gap that divides the rich from the poor in America," doing injury to that idealistic image of the nation portrayed by J. Hector St. John (Michel de Crèvecoeur) who, in his *Letters from an American Farmer* (1782), had seen in the United States a model of equity in which an economic leveling among the citizenry had obliterated the outdated European class system and substituted in its place a relatively classless society. In this new kind of society each person possessed a sufficiency; the castles and huts that characterized the old order were replaced by simple but adequate homes whose similarity to one another bespoke the economic leveling that had been achieved in what was essentially an agrarian economy.

In substituting a new and darker image – that of the mansion contrasted with the slum – industrial "progress" had severely damaged the ideals in which America had once taken such pride. "What were these things called democracy and equality about which all men prated?" asked Dreiser. He heard "constant palaver about the equality of opportunity" that was supposed to characterize American life, but he saw little evidence that it was being taken seriously. Men preached one thing and practiced another. Self-interest appeared to be the only guiding interest of men, and the practical results of this for Dreiser were disheartening in the extreme. Everywhere he went, from Chicago to Saint Louis, to Pittsburgh, to New York City, he "seemed everywhere to sense either a terrifying desire for lust or pleasure or wealth, accompanied by a heartlessness which was freezing to the soul, or a dogged resignation to deprivation and misery." In New York City this dichotomy was epitomized by the show and luxury of "Millionaire's Row" on upper Fifth Avenue, where men such as Vanderbilt and Yerkes had raised their marble palaces, contrasted with the Bowery and its "endless line of degraded and impossible lodging houses, a perfect whorl of bums and failures," with citizens sleeping over gratings or in doorways or entrances to cellars.

"All I could think of was that since nature would or could not do anything for man, he must, if he could, do something for himself," wrote Dreiser in 1922. But the 1920s, of all periods, were a time when business rode high and relatively unchallenged, when even the president, Calvin Coolidge, could announce that "the business of America is business." The inherently revolutionary subtext of all of Dreiser's novels, with their challenge to the capitalistic system itself, would not be much noted until a later time, at least until after the financial debacle of 1929 had plunged the nation into the Great Depression.

Meanwhile, those who sensed the radical nature of Dreiser's fiction and found it disturbing in ways that they may not have fully or even consciously comprehended, but who recognized the threatening validity of the economic message that lay just beneath the events in his stories, would find it both safer and simpler to attack him at his weakest point, his control of literary style. The overriding objective seems to have been to demolish the threat Dreiser presented, and for most hostile critics this was to be accomplished most easily by attacking him on artistic grounds. Therefore, the debate that centered on his ability or inability to produce an English sentence that was coherent, let alone beautiful, was a diversionary maneuver. It served actually to camouflage a reaction against his writing that had its foundation in dimly perceived yet dearly held economic theories that were sacrosanct and not to be challenged.

Given the impetus of war – always a catalyst for change – after the armistice of 1918 American manners and mores altered rather drastically, and this general loosening of the strictures upon behavior, during what came to be known as the Jazz Age, served to reduce considerably the emphasis upon the questionable morality of Dreiser's characters. The official censors were no less busily occupied than previously, but since Dreiser published no new novel until 1925, the debate over his work cooled somewhat, freezing both opponents and adherents in positions taken earlier. Then the appearance of *An American Tragedy* again brought his fiction to the fore. This time there was considerably less caviling with his frankly stated picture of life and even with his language. No less a critic than Stuart Sherman, who had condemned Dreiser's earlier work, was moved to praise this mammoth new piece of fiction. Soon came the rumors, helped along by Dreiser himself, that his name might be put up for the Nobel Prize.

In the same year as *An American Tragedy*, Burton Rascoe, a young midwestern journalist, produced the first book devoted to Dreiser. *Theodore Dreiser*, a slim volume composed to fit the format of the Modern American Writers Series published by McBride, dealt with both critical and biographical matters. Within a context that explored the vast changes produced in the America of 1850 by massive alterations in our national manner of living, changes largely the result of industrialization, Rascoe found all of Dreiser's novels to be "faithful mirrors of the national soul during the first phase" of industrial change. "Until Mr. Dreiser came along," declared Rascoe, "no one had had the wit to see the epical quality of this aspect of the drama of American life or the genius to translate it into terms of the novel." A generous report, Rascoe's book alluded to Dreiser's "force, power, and vision," to his "vast prodding energy," and to "his troubled sense of the human tragedy underlying this great play of forces."[5] Especially because it was written before *An American Tragedy* was available, Rascoe's defense of Dreiser seems courageous as well as directly on the mark. Understandably, he and the novelist became fast friends and enjoyed a lifetime association.

Reassessments: 1930-1940

Dreiser's reputation was not helped much by his literary inactivity during the 1930s (a time when a strong antiestablishment novel might have brought raves from politically minded critics). And the weak show made during the 1940s by his final books, *The Bulwark* and *The Stoic,* would only seem to confirm the opinions of those who preferred to dismiss him as a serious contender for literary honors. Scattered here and there, voices were heard that suggested a reassessment: Vernon L. Parrington, Ludwig Lewisohn, Clifton Fadiman, Granville Hicks, V. F. Calverton, James T. Farrell, and others. In 1932 Dorothy Dudley published her unusual study, *Forgotten Frontiers: Dreiser and the Land of the Free.* Having had the advantage of working directly with Dreiser, who gave her access to many of his papers, including his correspondence, and having been hugely impressed not only with the man's work but with Dreiser himself, Dudley's approach is one of frank adoration. That tone – as well as Dudley's highly personal style – is apparent even in her introductory chapter:

> He is an American high water-mark, capable of waves that fall beyond. . . . His story reflects the story of Americans – big waves washing high on the shores of history, and washing away some of the old orchards and farms. . . . He is to this day a challenge to writers to sacrifice themselves as completely, and more intimately if they can, to our history. He is large more than intimate. Yet he has passages, too, of identity with the mood, moments of penetration, when he goes over from being the historian into being the poet. In him our disorderly order gleams with its mysteries. He says of himself, "The riddle remains. I have solved nothing." (Dudley, 3-4)

Dudley's is the first study to examine Dreiser's life in depth and to relate it to his fiction. By this time, two autobiographies dealing with Dreiser's childhood were available, *A Hoosier Holiday* (1916) and *Dawn* (1931). Being well attuned to the modern psychological truism that decrees the child the father of the man, Dudley was much interested in seeking out revelations from Dreiser's earliest years and seeing in them the germs of later fictional episodes and themes. In addition, she had the advantage of numerous conversations with her subject, so that she may – and often does – refer to such colloquies. "One night I heard Dreiser speaking of his mother," is typical of

statements leading into passages that quote directly from her conversations with Dreiser; among the permanent contributions of this
book are the novelist's statements of fact and opinion that appear
only here. Dudley's book is undocumented, unfortunately; we must
take her word for what she wrote. But the fact that Dreiser had
opportunity to read and approve the manuscript lends the volume a
considerable degree of authority.

Here and there amid the critical commentary appeared a handful
of reasoned attempts to place Dreiser appropriately within the
context of American literary history. Perhaps the most equitable was
that written by one of the professorial clan so scorned by Mencken:
Russell Blankenship of Whitman College. In his comprehensive
American Literature as an Expression of the National Mind (1931),
Blankenship attempted to mete out justice to Dreiser in terms of his
biography, his literary method, his philosophy, and, ultimately, his
significance. He identified Dreiser accurately as being "the most
consistent and uncompromising exponent of naturalism" in America,
past or present, tracing that consistency of approach as it was
employed in novels from *Sister Carrie* through *An American
Tragedy.*[6] Although constantly seeking for certainty, comfort, and the
sense of satisfaction that comes from being sure about the purpose
of life, Dreiser is said to be, temperamentally, a skeptic. Not only is
he uncertain about what life really is but, adds Blankenship, he is not
even certain that he is uncertain; despite Dreiser's immense curiosity
concerning the spectacle of life as it lies all about him, ever shifting
and changing its surface, the riddle of existence withholds its inner-
most secrets.

Blankenship takes notice of Dreiser's journalistic beginnings, but
he probes no deeper than to blame that apprenticeship for the lack
of elegance in Dreiser's style, which, in the cliché of the day, he finds
to be "wholly devoid of grace and subtlety," at times deserving even
the barren epithet *poor.* On the other hand, and somewhat surprisingly, Blankenship is insightful – and courageous – enough to
suggest that "Dreiser's style in general is a good one for Dreiser," his
method being in harmony with his subject matter in its structure and
diction. As a whole then, Dreiser turns out to be "a much more
effective writer" than many of his critics make him out to be, a
considerably better stylist than if he had taken the advice offered "by
all the teachers of English composition." The note sounded here was

something new and foreshadowed notions that would not surface for another two decades and more.

On the matter of Dreiser's all-around importance, Blankenship was forthright: "Dreiser is by far the most significant writer now working in the American field. . . . he is the most powerful, and from the standpoint of literary development he is the most significant. . . . Almost unaided, [he] has brought current American fiction into harmony with the tone of contemporary life [which] so admirably lends itself to naturalistic treatment that it can be said almost to demand such presentation" (Blankenship, 540).

Less than two decades after Stuart Sherman had excoriated Dreiser for daring to suggest that American society could ever have any possible relationship to the naturalistic philosophy of life, another voice expresses the polar opposite – again, intimations of things to come.

A Major Writer: 1940-1950

During the 1940s Dreiser began to come into his own as a novelist of great and enduring significance. Most important in a critical sense, probably because its youthful author went on to establish an important career as an authority on American literature, was the defense of Dreiser and what he stood for presented in Alfred Kazin's *On Native Grounds* (1942). Dealing with Dreiser's career in the context of his times as seen in retrospect by a member of the younger generation (Kazin was born in 1915, the year Dreiser published *The "Genius"*), the critic set out to explode what he called "the folkloric myth" that Dreiser was bereft of everything except genius. Instead, he placed Dreiser among the great "folk writers," beside Homer and Whitman. In a final judgment he called the novelist "stronger than all the others of his time, and at the same time more poignant; greater than the world he has described, but as significant as the people in it."[7]

Following Dreiser's death in 1946 and the flurry of critical comment that accompanied it, the basis for a genuine reassessment was set in 1949 by the publication of Robert H. Elias's *Theodore Dreiser: Apostle of Nature*. Here for the first time Dreiser was approached by a serious literary scholar of the new generation, who, like Kazin, was young enough not to have been adversely biased by the early battles over Dreiser's books. In addition, Elias had worked directly with Dreiser for a number of years prior to his death and had been given access to the novelist's papers, including his correspondence. The result was a critical biography, sympathetic but reasoned in its approach, which for more than 40 years has served as a cornerstone for Dreiser studies.

One advantage of having at hand the Dreiser papers – they had gone to the University of Pennsylvania, where Elias taught, in 1942 – was that Elias need not rely solely on the rapidly aging and self-protective Dreiser or even on his published autobiographies for data. For more complete and accurate accounts and for the personal names that had needed to be disguised during Dreiser's lifetime, Elias could refer to the handwritten manuscripts of *Dawn, A Hoosier Holiday,* and *Newspaper Days,* the latter being (c. 1930) the amended title of *A Book about Myself.* Elias probed Dreiser's childhood and young manhood for their significance concerning the novelist's philosophy as expressed in his fiction, and he interjected his considered interpretation of events. Here, for instance, is young Dreiser in Pittsburgh during the spring of 1894, on the verge of discovering the first book to overwhelm him with its significance in unlocking the puzzle called life:

> As he searched for answers, he groped for formulas, but formulas always appeared to ignore the questions and left him, eventually, certain only that life was bewilderingly complex. . . . [He] was caught up by the currents and carried along while he wondered and speculated about them, observing the baffled gropings of others who were more deeply immersed in the destructive element. He wanted primarily to be superior to those who were sucked down in vortex and undertow; he wanted to be secure and to understand what it was that made life precarious. He wanted to find some recognition somewhere that verbal nostrums were inadequate for man's condition. (Elias 1949, 71-73)

No writer, of course, had yet dealt with Dreiser's later and final years, and because of his close contact and his visits to Dreiser's Hollywood home, Elias was superbly equipped to treat this aspect of Dreiser's life. Among the facts he brought forth was the amazing and somewhat confounding news that Dreiser, always the gruff opponent of conventional religion – the agnostic, the atheist, even – this same Dreiser in his final year, on a series of Sundays, "went to church, not always the same church, but some church, whether Congregational or Christian Scientist, and on Good Friday 1945 he was so moved by the service he attended that he took communion and left deeply shaken by the experience" (Elias 1949, 298). Elias's biography, without any doubt, capped all efforts in Dreiser studies during the 1940s and, indeed, during the first half of the century. Updated and amended in its 1970 revision, it continues to serve Dreiser scholars well.

Chapter Nine

The Growth of Dreiser's Reputation: 1950-1980

Dreiser's genius [was] discovering something major which no writer had thus far rendered.

– Larzer Ziff, 1966

Reappraisals: The 1950s

The turnaround in Dreiser's critical esteem was by no means immediate. What was important was that the appraisals of recent American literature that emerged during the 1950s were characterized by a considerable reduction in critical hostility, by a more widespread understanding and acceptance of what Dreiser actually had done, and by new insights and interpretations that paved the way for still greater understanding and acceptance.

In 1951 critic-historian Van Wyck Brooks reversed an unsympathetic opinion offered in 1918 by depicting the Dreiser contribution much more positively in his book *The Confident Years: 1885-1915.* Brooks now began a major chapter with praise for *Sister Carrie* and *Jennie Gerhardt,* both of which, he said, "brimmed over with a sense of the wonder, the colour and the beauty of life, and its cruelty, rank favouritism, uncertainty, indifference and sorrow," qualities that triumphed over Dreiser's "flat-footed, unleavened, [and] elephantine" style of writing. One could not expect unmitigated praise from Brooks, of course, whose stubborn conservatism was partly exemplified by his insistence upon being among the last Americans to retain the British ending *our* in words such as *colour* and *favour.* Admirers of Dreiser were happy enough to find Brooks willing to make remarks such as, "He never lost the sense of wonder, the ingenuousness, the candour that is, after all, with novelists, so essential and so rare."[1]

Also appearing in 1951 was the final work of F. O. Matthiessen, the admired author of *American Renaissance:* an examination of Dreiser's life and works entitled *Theodore Dreiser.* It took cognizance of the long-standing battle concerning Dreiser and his books and defended the novelist on the basis of his painfully truthful depiction of things he had experienced and observed, calling him a writer who sees no model for the type of thing he wants to do, and so becomes "a primary example of the frequent American need to begin all over again from scratch." He dubbed Dreiser an "authentic primitive," an original artist, "not unlike the occasional American sign painter who has found that he possessed the dogged skills to create a portrait likeness, and then has bent all the force of a rugged character to realize this verity." Himself a noted social critic, Matthiessen very understandably emphasized Dreiser's concern for the unhealthy directions taken by American society. As a result, his book contains the first methodical attempt to deal with Dreiser's political attitudes and in that chapter, "Dreiser's Politics," Matthiessen summarizes a stance that had been shaped early and held until death: "[Dreiser] had slowly learned the lesson that there could be no humane life in the United States until the inequities should be removed that had thwarted or destroyed so many of the characters in his fiction."[2]

Maxwell Geismar in *Rebels and Ancestors* (1953), which summarized roughly the same period of literary history as Brooks's *Confident Years,* presented Dreiser's as the ultimate career in a sequence of careers that included those of Frank Norris, Stephen Crane, Jack London, and Ellen Glasgow. For Geismar, rather than being a crude primitive, Dreiser actually produced books that operate on various levels of interpretation simultaneously. The first is always the story itself "with its sense of illusion and glamour." The second level is that on which Dreiser the author injects his own commentary concerning the events and people he is presenting, those brief (or lengthy) "editorial" passages every reader is aware of. The third level is "a still more profound and tragic level of psychological interpretation conveyed mainly by the development of the story itself."[3] It is on this third level, says Geismar, that Dreiser shows himself to be truly an artist, this level on which the reader, taking into consideration everything that has been displayed on the page, relates to character and fable, responding from his or her own personal orienta-

tion. To see Dreiser as an artist was something relatively new in
Dreiser studies; Geismar's effort pointed the way toward further and
even more flattering analyses.

Works by Kenneth Lynn and Charles Child Walcutt presented
Dreiser amid special contexts that would soon become standard
critical approaches to the man and his contribution. Lynn's title *The
Dream of Success* (1955) indicated his focus on the American dream
of "making it" in a wealth-oriented society, a theme exemplified in
the many rags-to-riches books by Horatio Alger. His chapter on
Dreiser opens with the following: "Theodore Dreiser asserted, with a
blunt directness which no other American writer at the turn of the
century could match, that pecuniary and sexual success were the
values of American society, that they were his values, too, and that
they were therefore worthy of his total attention as a literary artist."[4]
Lynn then reviews Dreiser's life and his novels from *Sister Carrie*
through *An American Tragedy*, with glances at the final novels as
well, developing the money and sex themes that he had identified as
being their motivating impulses. Walcutt, in *American Literary Naturalism, A Divided Stream* (1956), was among the first officially to
recognize that the "classic" phase of naturalistic writing had passed
and was ready to be analyzed as a discrete movement in American
literature.[5] Of all naturalistic writers in America, concluded Walcutt,
Dreiser produced the most powerful, the most moving novels. The
novelist's own view was split, says Walcutt, drawn on the one hand
toward the belief that earthly life had no meaning whatsoever and
responding on the other hand to a desperate need to believe that it
did possess true significance. Thus, Dreiser "is his own divided
stream of pity and guilt, of wonder and terror, of objectivity and
responsibility." From *Sister Carrie* to *The Stoic*, in this interpretation, Dreiser moved from his initial belief in the essential purpose-
lessness of life toward the notion that the exercise of one's will to
power (the superman theory) gave life meaning and zest, then
moved from this espousal of rugged individualism toward a conversion to socialism that was allied with the belief that the evils of society *can* be ameliorated, and ended (in *The Stoic*) by surrendering to
the powerful lure of the spirit, which "is not naturalism, after all."
What did not change, concludes Walcutt, was Dreiser's power as a
novelist. Both Lynn's and Walcutt's positions have, of course, given
rise to later refinements and refutations of the themes they explored.

Two of the women who loved Dreiser and aided him professionally made significant contributions during the 1950s. The first was his
widow, Helen Richardson Dreiser. In her memoir *My Life with
Dreiser* (1951), Helen told of her years (1919-1945) with the novelist
in a rather circumspect manner even as she revealed something new
concerning Dreiser's notorious promiscuity (the book was dedicated
to "the unknown women in the life of Theodore Dreiser, who
devoted themselves unselfishly to the beauty of his intellect and its
artistic unfoldment"). Helen and Theodore's years together were not
tranquil ones, and Helen makes no effort to remain objective in
recounting the frequent and often severe difficulties encountered in
living with a volatile artistic personality. Helen was typical of the
women who fell hard for Dreiser, and she describes her reaction to
meeting him in terms that set the tone for her book: "Theodore
Dreiser seemed to me to move in a large orbit and for me, at my age
and with my limited background, to have come into contact with a
man of his caliber was an astounding experience. . . . Life for me
during the next few days was a state of intoxicating anticipation, and
all preconceived plans of action were, for the time, discarded. At last
I had found a man whose response to beauty was deep and true"
(H. Dreiser, 24-25). In spite of great provocation, Helen remained
with Dreiser the remainder of his life. Their estrangements were
frequent and on occasion lengthy, but she always returned to him.
Her book has been a valuable addition to the records of Dreiser's
personal life. It has contributed much also to our knowledge of
Dreiser's creative life, in particular his years in Hollywood after 1919,
while he helped Helen to establish a career in the movies. Helen was
involved in his research for *An American Tragedy,* and during his
final years, again in Hollywood, she was beside him while he struggled in the face of declining powers to complete *The Bulwark* and
The Stoic.

Louise Campbell of Philadelphia had been Dreiser's lover and
volunteer editor during the while he worked on *The Financier* and
The Titan, and she maintained the connection, at least in her editorial capacity, until Dreiser died. In 1959 she published a slim volume
called *Letters to Louise* in which she recounts the professional side
of their relationship, gathering together in a narrative framework the
letters Dreiser wrote to her, preserving these and opening a door for
students into Dreiser's authorial methods. Had Campbell been as

open regarding her romantic alliance as she was regarding her editorial assistance, her book could have been a truly major contribution. But the public had to wait for Dreiser's own diaries, published 30 years later, to learn the details of the love affair, which was one of the most significant in Dreiser's life.

Special aspects of Dreiser's work were now beginning to receive attention by writers such as Blanche H. Gelfant, who dealt with Dreiser's fiction within the context of the "city novel," and Walter Blackstock, who pointed out the significant interaction in Dreiser's fiction between beauty and money. Joseph J. Kwiat linked Dreiser with American artists of the Ash Can school, who were contemporaries of Dreiser; like him, these painters – Luks, Sloan, Glackens, and others – had once been reviled and only later found recognition. Kwiat demonstrated that what the Ash Can artists had accomplished with subject and technique should rightly be seen as the graphic-arts equivalent of Dreiser's accomplishment in fiction.

The study of Dreiser's work and career was facilitated in 1955 by publication of *The Stature of Theodore Dreiser,* the first collection of critical materials to attempt a survey in toto of the man and his work. Edited by Alfred Kazin and Charles Shapiro, this volume was motivated by the evolving knowledge that from the earliest days of his career as a novelist Dreiser had been in one manner or another recognized as constituting a drastic break with the genteel tradition, "a whole new class, a tendency, a disturbing movement in American life, an eruption from below"(5). In documenting this "eruption," the editors brought together a number of early portraits of Dreiser by writers who had known him, such as Edgar Lee Masters and Ford Madox Ford, as well as professional correspondence between Dreiser and James T. Farrell.

Here for the first time turn-of-the-century reviews of *Sister Carrie* were reprinted, allowing fans of that novel to see precisely what had been said of it upon its publication in 1900. "The Barbaric Naturalism of Mr. Dreiser" and "The Dreiser Bugaboo," those 1915-era essays with which Stuart P. Sherman and H. L. Mencken had launched the critical battle over Dreiser's contribution, were included, and a solid collection of disparate essays gathered from across the historical spectrum made a reader aware of the considerable disagreement that had accompanied Dreiser's career and of the penetrating studies of his fiction that had been published separately

up to the 1950s. With this book, the student now possessed a minia-
ture library calculated to inform him or her about Dreiser the man
and Dreiser the writer in a generalized yet well-rounded and
balanced manner. An inclusive bibliography helped to guide the
reader to more specialized investigations. Particularly when paired
with later critical collections, *The Stature of Theodore Dreiser*
continues to serve a valuable purpose.

As the decade closed, Robert H. Elias published another major
contribution to Dreiser studies, a three-volume edition of *Letters of
Theodore Dreiser* (1959). This collection, the first (and still the only)
sizable printing of Dreiser's correspondence with dozens of his
contemporaries, at once became indispensable to those interested in
the novelist's life and career.

Blossoming: The 1960s

The importance of Dreiser's being seen in new contexts cannot be
overestimated. This change helped to dissipate the old and stubborn
objections to his work even as it wrenched his novels out of the
moral-political morass in which they had tended to mire down
during the second decade of the century. From now on, the arguments both for and against Dreiser's importance would need to rest
on different ground. One result of these revisionist studies of America and its writers was a spate of new books during the 1960s. All of
them were written by critics younger even than Kazin, all were free
of hostile bias, and all of them inevitably reflected the new ways of
approaching Dreiser, his novels, and his place in the tradition. These
books, by such writers as Charles Shapiro, John McAleer, and
Richard Lehan, were devoted to Dreiser exclusively, and each
reflected the influence of new biographical data unearthed by Elias
and added to by others. Helen Dreiser's story, for instance, was
supplemented by another long-time friend, admirer, lover, and
volunteer editor, Marguerite Tjader, who presented a contrasting, if
equally subjective, viewpoint in *Theodore Dreiser: A New Dimension*
(1965). The book was of particular relevance to those interested in
Dreiser's final years in Hollywood, where he attempted to complete
The Bulwark and *The Stoic* while juggling his relationships with both
Helen and Marguerite. Tjader tells of her first encounter with
Dreiser, in 1928, and her feeling that "here was a human being,

supersensitive; a doctor of souls, knowing them and seeing their secrets. . . . his presence radiating some kind of glow. . . . his mind [seeming] like an open plain across which he could gallop or cavort in any direction."[6] Of special importance are Tjader's record of her associations with Dreiser during the 1930s, when she knew him best; her personal account of his final visit to New York in May 1944, to receive the Award of Merit medal from the American Academy of Arts and Letters; and her memories of her residence in Hollywood, where she helped Dreiser complete *The Bulwark* and attempting to help him finish *The Stoic* (for which, among other services, she visited the tomb of Charles T. Yerkes in Brooklyn's Greenwood Cemetery and sent in her first-hand report). Glossed over in this subjective account is Tjader's falling out with Helen Dreiser, who also wished to be important in completing *The Stoic,* and the bitter quarrels that ensued. But the book adds much of value to the biographical record, one more piece in the mosaic that gradually was building.

In terms of biography, the central event of the 1960s without doubt was the publication in mid-decade of W. R. Swanberg's massive *Dreiser,* the first study by a professional biographer and the first to mine the Dreiser Collection in Philadelphia for everything it could offer concerning the writer's life (literary criticism not being Swanberg's aim). It has been common of late, particularly among Dreiser scholars, to deprecate the Swanberg biography by pointing out that it was undertaken not so much by choice as by assignment and that Swanberg proved unable to conceal his growing antipathy for his subject as his investigation and writing progressed. Not sharing these sentiments altogether and seeing the resultant work less as a portrait in distaste than as an effort to reveal the truth, however unflattering, I come to different conclusions regarding *Dreiser.* It remains – and seems likely to remain for some time to come – the most complete account, an omnibus in the blockbuster tradition. It answers nearly any question the ordinary reader might wish to ask. It is literally crammed with data deriving not only from primary documents in the Dreiser archives but from Swanberg's wide correspondence and from personal interviews conducted with dozens of Dreiser's contemporaries and close friends. These interviews in particular, so many accomplished shortly before the subjects' deaths, by themselves represent an accomplishment whose true value may not be adequately realized for decades. While there is always room for a "different" biography, especially a revisionist one, Swanberg's *Dreiser* is the book against which all newcomers will be measured against.

A further portion of the biographical record was filled in by Ruth Kennell, who in 1927 served as Dreiser's secretary-guide on his 66-day tour of the Soviet Union (the basis for his book *Dreiser Looks at Russia*). *Theodore Dreiser and the Soviet Union* (1969) is Kennell's record of that adventure, from her vantage point. But when Dreiser's own diary of the trip is finally published, it will be seen that at a great many points it was Kennell who wrote the diary entries, albeit at Dreiser's direction. Kennell's record is still valuable, however, and she supplements her story with accounts of Dreiser's social and political action during the 1930s, when he crusaded actively in support of Tom Mooney, the convicted anarchist, the oppressed coal miners of Harlan County, Kentucky, and the Scottsboro boys, black youths accused of rape in the deep South. In the final chapters, Kennell discusses the continuation of Dreiser's support of progressive causes through World War II. Anyone interested in Dreiser's political activities will profit from studying Kennell's book.

Swanberg's biography was joined four years later by a pair of books that are of supreme importance in establishing a new reputation for Theodore Dreiser. The first of these, edited by Jackson R. Bryer, was *Fifteen Modern American Authors*, an assessment of biographical and critical materials concerning those writers generally agreed to have excelled since 1900, each separate assessment taking the form of an essay by a recognized expert on the writer concerned. *Fifteen Modern American Authors*, so far as Dreiser was concerned, carried a twofold significance. It conferred upon him the official academic "seal of approval," an honor long withheld. He was now placed where he rightly belonged, among his peers, in company with Cather, Eliot, Faulkner, Fitzgerald, Frost, Hemingway, O'Neill, and other acknowledged "greats" of the modern era. For the timid, no further equivocation was now required; it was "okay" to like Dreiser, to read his books, to study his *oeuvre*, and to write about him. Also, the essay on Dreiser's career, fittingly composed by Robert Elias, proved to be a masterpiece, tracing critical and biographical interest in Dreiser from its earliest dates, assessing and comparing as it went, and not ignoring the burgeoning interest in far-flung spots such as Scandinavia, Germany, France, Italy, Russia, and Japan. Updated in

1973 as *Sixteen Modern American Authors* (to include William Carlos Williams) and again in 1990 (this time with the Dreiser update done by James L. W. West III), this volume has become a major reference that keeps pace with scholarly developments.

During the same year (1969) this comprehensive evaluation of scholarship was joined by another pacesetting volume, *Two Dreisers*, by Ellen Moers. In this case, a literary critic trained in modern methodology came upon Dreiser, by accident apparently, after arriving at her maturity. Tremendously impressed by what she saw in his pages, Moers proceeded to delve more deeply into the texts and biographical-historical circumstances surrounding Dreiser's two admitted masterworks, *Sister Carrie* and *An American Tragedy*. The result was a book of a wholly new sort, one that brought to light many of the basic source materials for ideas that motivated the novels and explained their significance, tying Dreiser to contemporaries such as Stephen Crane, William Dean Howells, and Elmer Gates, as well as to the painters of the Ash Can school, to early photographers such as Alfred Stieglitz, and to contemporary psychoanalysts such as A. A. Brill. In her eyes, Dreiser became incomparably more complex as man and writer than anyone had imagined, possessed of a finesse that, Moers felt, placed him in the company of Yeats, Joyce, Shaw, Proust, Stravinsky, and even Picasso. Robert Elias, by now the dean of Dreiser scholars, said that Moers had caused "biography and criticism [to] strengthen each other and open a new path to Dreiser."[7]

The notion that Dreiser might be something more than an ill- and semi-taught journalist with delusions of grandeur had been suggested in 1952 by Alexander Kern in his article "Dreiser's Difficult Beauty," and that dissenting view was carried further not only by Ellen Moers but also, during the 1960s, by William Phillips, who in his "The Imagery of Dreiser's Novels" analyzed the patterns of metaphor and symbolism moving through the novels to indicate that the author, whatever his shortcomings, was capable of a controlled, behind-the-scenes manipulation of subtle elements that worked successfully to reinforce his philosophical concepts. Richard Poirier's *A World Elsewhere* (1966), devoted to an investigation of the place of style in American literature since James Fenimore Cooper, declared that one of the jobs of American authors was to rid themselves and America of styles imposed on them by history.[8] Only by so doing could they then reshape language and literature to suit their own personal visions of a new society. Critics from 1915 to 1935 would be shocked, no doubt, to find Dreiser placed here in the company of such respected stylists as Emerson, Hawthorne, Whitman, Thoreau, Twain, James, Fitzgerald, and Faulkner. But Poirier has reasons, and he argues them well.

Dreiser, he says, was instinctively aware that in America personal relationships counted for less than did the overwhelming and immutable forces that both shaped and determined events in the emerging urban complexes making up the America he knew and understood. For Dreiser, the city was the immense force that bound people together in America, and it was impersonal. Therefore, in Dreiser's novels, a reader should not be surprised that the attention given personal relationships often seems scant compared to the attention lavished on the panoramic quality of the city itself, that great, humming industrial mechanism that was becoming more and more the typical American environment. The inarticulate quality of Dreiser's characters is quite appropriate, suggests Poirier, for persons accustomed less to speaking their thoughts than to taking things in with their eyes – the type of dumb wonderment, for instance, with which Carrie Meeber confronts 1889 Chicago. "The floods of language by which [Dreiser] embraces things outside himself are a verbal equivalent to the visual obsessions of his characters," says Poirier. And so, like other major American writers before him, Dreiser intuitively created a new style for new experiences, one that was not less legitimate than styles that prevailed during the previous century, but only different. For Poirier, Dreiser "belongs in the strongest tradition of American literature [and] in his blatant strangeness he redefines some filaments of that tradition for us" (Poirer, 249).

High Tide: The 1970s

That "new path to Dreiser" of which Elias had spoken was cleared further and the route facilitated almost at once by a pair of events occurring as the decade of the 1970s opened. The first of these was the establishment of *The Dreiser Newsletter,* under the editorship of Richard W. Dowell and Robert P. Saalbach, on the Terre Haute campus of Indiana State University. Terre Haute had never honored its native son, although it had made something of a patron saint out of his brother Paul, innocuous popular songs apparently being more digestible than naturalistic novels. Something in the way of amends was attempted by establishment of the *Newsletter*, with a roster of Dreiser scholars corralled into service as contributing editors: Hening Cohen, Philip Gerber, Richard Lehan, John McAleer, Donald Pizer, Claude M. Simpson, Jr., and Neda Westlake, curator of the Dreiser Collection in Philadelphia. In the biannual issues of the *Newsletter*, those interested in Dreiser possessed a forum for essays, reviews, interviews, notes, and queries. The publication also provided a method for keeping abreast of dissertations and theses on Dreiser and related topics, and Frederic E. Rusch began an annual checklist of bibliographical items bearing upon Dreiser, which included, as they appeared, new editions and reprints of Dreiser's works. Through the years, other Dreiser scholars have taken their turns as contributing editors: Jack Salzman, Ellen Moers, Robert P. Saalbach, Lawrence E. Hussman, Thomas P. Riggio, T. D. Nostwich, and James L. W. West, III. The *Newsletter* (which in 1987 changed its title to *Dreiser Studies*) has at one time or another printed the views and opinions of just about every scholar working on Dreiser, and an impressive percentage of books on Dreiser trace their beginnings to essays printed in its pages. After 1977 Richard Dowell continued as sole editor, relinquishing his post in 1990 after 20 years of service to Frederic Rusch, who previously had served on the staff as official bibliographer.

In 1971 the Department of English at Terre Haute sponsored a festival commemorating the one-hundredth birthday of Theodore Dreiser. The Dreiser Centennial, as it has come to be known, marked the first formal gathering of persons interested in Dreiser and his works and included presentations by a number of those most active in Dreiser studies: Philip Gerber, Richard Lehan, Rolf Lunden, John McAleer, Ellen Moers, Robert Saalbach, Charles Shapiro, and Neda Westlake. Ruth Kennell and Marguerite Tjader gave presentations based upon their personal involvement with Dreiser as assistants in his work during the 1920s and 1930s.

Evening entertainments were offered by Tedi Dreiser, Theodore's grandniece, in a series of Paul Dresser songs, and by the theater department of the university, which presented Dreiser's play *The Girl in the Coffin*. In addition to the speakers, the Centennial was notable for bringing together a number of Dreiser family members, including his niece Dr. Vera Dreiser, as well as old friends such as the painter Gilbert Wilson, who had known – and been helped by – Dreiser in the 1930s. Foreign representatives included, most notably, Professor Yassen Zassoursky of the University of Moscow, reminding the gathering of the wide popularity and circulation of Dreiser's novels in the Soviet Union.

A number of important aids to Dreiser scholarship appeared during the 1970s, beginning in 1971 with John Lydenberg's *Dreiser: A Collection of Critical Essays,* which gathered essays published between 1915 and 1964, many of them salient chapters from books by writers such as Kazin, Cowley, Mencken, Fiedler, Howe, and Moers. In the following year Jack Salzman published his monumental *Theodore Dreiser: The Critical Reception,* based in part on the clipping files in the Dreiser Collection. For each of Dreiser's books, nonfiction as well as fiction, Salzman reprinted the reviews that had appeared at the time in newspapers and magazines, so far as they could be located. With this volume at hand, a student need take no one else's word for what the contemporary reception of the various books had been.

In 1975 the most complete bibliography appeared, edited by Donald Pizer, Richard W. Dowell, and Frederic E. Rusch. The book went far beyond any of the bibliographies and checklists heretofore published, many of which were specialized or fragmentary. Among works by Dreiser, the editors listed books and pamphlets, contributions to books, pamphlets, and periodicals, including newspapers, miscellaneous publications, published letters, interviews and speeches, and also provided a section on library holdings of Dreiser manuscripts. Among works on Dreiser were listed the previous bibliographies and checklists, books, pamphlets, portions of books, newspapers and journal articles, reviews, tapes, and a list of theses and dissertations on Dreiser. A final section was devoted to a listing of productions of Dreiser's plays and of adaptations – usually intended for the motion pictures – of his novels and stories. A work designed for the student, Philip Gerber's *Plots and Characters in the Fiction of Theodore Dreiser* appeared in 1977, summarizing the stories contained in the novels and short stories and providing capsule descriptions of all the characters who inhabit them.

Of the critical books devoted to Dreiser during the 1970s, the first to appear was Robert Penn Warren's *Homage to Theodore Dreiser*, timed to coincide with Dreiser's centennial in 1971. Here was praise from a highly respected member of the literary community, a modern master of both fiction and poetry, and perhaps an unlikely admirer of Dreiser's work. But Warren, who prefaced his book with a pair of original poems centered on Dreiser, revealed that he had read all of Dreiser's novels through the years, not always wholly convinced at the time of their quality – except for *An American Tragedy*, which he had admired from the time he first read it. But he had found that the novels stuck in his mind, were ineradicable, especially the Cowperwood trilogy. They made their impression, and it was a lasting one. In *Homage*, he sets out to demolish the time-honored cliché of Dreiser as "a kind of uninspired recorder blundering along in a dreary effort to transcribe actuality" and to replace it with his considered opinion that the man was an artist whose method in dealing with actuality was so direct, so precise, that his surfaces too often concealed the art that produced them. Referring often to the work of scholars who had helped elucidate the significance of the novels, Warren ultimately sees Dreiser as "a powerful artist," America's chief "philosopher of 'illusion,' " a writer whose novels "touched nerves that led deep into American life."[9]

W. M. Frohock in 1972 and James Lundquist in 1974 produced concise studies, both entitled *Theodore Dreiser*, which continued and extended the tradition established by Gerber and McAleer during the 1960s. Following these came a larger and more ambitious study by Donald Pizer, *The Novels of Theodore Dreiser* (1976), which offered penetrating analyses of the novels, described the conditions under which they were composed, and traced their sources. Pizer's was the major critical study to appear during the decade. In a different vein, that same year, Dr. Vera Dreiser published her biographical study, *My Uncle Theodore*. A clinical psychologist, she wrote from within the complicated family context in which Dreiser necessarily existed. Vera was the daughter of Dreiser's brother Ed; her mother had been a close friend of Sara White, Dreiser's first wife. Vera met her illustrious uncle in 1922 when she was 14, at a soiree given by Mame Dreiser Brennan. It was a tense evening for her parents, who disapproved of the novelist's alliance with Helen Richardson (whom Dreiser escorted to the party), but a time of great excitement for Vera, who was full of adolescent curiosity concerning "why [her uncle's] life's affairs were unmentionable in our home, and why my mother disliked him so intensely."[10] The book is replete with family lore, to which Vera Dreiser adds her own psychological interpretation of her uncle's personality, finding that he had never quite outgrown the dominance of his mother in his affections, and thus had remained in many ways childlike, his emotional development arrested. In addition, she identified Theodore as being somewhat paranoid and functionally schizophrenic, diagnoses with which many students of Dreiser have disagreed. But the new biographical facts (and family photographs) give the book lasting value, whatever one's opinion might be of the analysis of personality.

The work of providing readers with Dreiser texts that had never been published – or texts that had to all intents and purposes been "lost" since their original, ephemeral printings, usually in newspapers or in periodicals long since suspended – was carried out by John J. McAleer and Dreiser's long-time friend Marguerite Tjader. Together they undertook the Herculean task of producing an accurate and representative yet manageable text from the immense collection of philosophical manuscripts on which Dreiser had lavished much time and effort during his middle years. Begun during the 1930s and never completed (although here and there along the way a few separate essays had been polished and made their way into print), these philosophical statements had languished unseen. Dreiser's ambitious intention had been to include everything of importance concerning the nature of human life that he was able to cast into words. He saw these essays, when completed and published, as constituting the nonfiction equivalent of his novels and stories.

One of the largest surprises in Dreiser studies has been that Dreiser, despite prolific publication during his lifetime – 26 volumes, many of them of extreme length – published only a fraction of his actual composition. At his death, Dreiser's widow estimated that the philosophical manuscripts alone, if stacked, would reach the ceiling of her California living room. They came to the Dreiser Collection in 11 boxes, and a young scholar, Sydney Horovitz, made an initial attempt to categorize the essays and arrange them, with an eye to potential publication. Upon Horovitz's untimely death, the project remained in limbo until Marguerite Tjader, who knew from personal experience the high priority Dreiser always assigned these "Notes on Life," as he called them, felt impelled to take up the task. She knew first-hand of Dreiser's intention to shape a book from the manuscripts and she believed strongly in its value, not only to students of Dreiser's fiction but to the American reading public.

The result was a volume that revealed much about the influence on Dreiser of thinkers such as Herbert Spencer, whose *First Principles* (1862) had originally – as early as 1894 – set his brain whirling with a desire to comprehend life and to explain it, and Jacques Loeb, the impact of whose *The Mechanistic Conception of Life* (1912) could be discerned even in certain titles among the pile of essays: "The Mechanism Called the Universe," "The Mechanism Called Life," and "The Mechanism Called Man." Dreiser's original thinking, drawn from his lifetime of experiences and observations, was joined with influences such as these to explain the strong role played in life by the force of illusion and by the various "myths" he saw as comprising the modern – meaning here the *American* – approach to existence, myths such as those of Individuality, Free Will, Creative Power, Individual Possession, and Individual Responsibility.

From the beginning, the texts of Dreiser's novels had been peppered with philosophical comments and asides. Clearly he was driven to comprehend what he so often termed the beauty and the wonder and the terror of human existence. He desperately needed to make sense out of what all too often appeared to be no more than an incoherent, chaotic, confusing, and perhaps even unconnected series of occurrences, physical and mental and spiritual, which we call life. In his own bewilderment and dark, brooding sense of being continually acted on by unopposable forces rather than acting freely, Dreiser came close at times to giving up any hope of understanding life. When not engaged in his sanity-saving efforts to make philosophical sense out of the span of time elapsing between cradle and grave, he was likely to retreat into inchoate images not unlike those offered by his contemporary and fellow truthseeker, Eugene O'Neill: "Our lives are merely strange dark interludes in the electrical display of God the Father!"[11] The appearance in 1974 of the Tjader-McAleer edition, appropriately retaining Dreiser's working title *Notes on Life*, made it possible for scholars to gain easy access to the full degree of thinking accomplished by the novelist during his lifetime and to accept it or to reject it as each chose.

From abroad, the Indian scholar R. N. Mookerjee offered *Theodore Dreiser: His Thought and Social Criticism* (1974), which treats a variety of influences such as family, religion, education, and journalistic training on Dreiser's social attitudes as expressed particularly during the last two decades of his life. Mookerjee's thesis concerns the importance of the American environment and its prevalent ideas to a proper comprehension of the man and his thought. From Sweden came a pair of books by Rolf Lunden. The first, *The Inevitable Equation* (1973), returns to the influence on Dreiser of Herbert Spencer's *First Principles* and the theory that "life" was characterized by pairs of balanced opposites such as the laws of supply and demand, antitheses that ended always in "equation." Those who perceive splits in Dreiser's own actions and beliefs can find support for those notions here. The second of Lunden's books, *Dreiser Looks at Scandinavia* (1977), concentrates on Dreiser's visit to the Scandinavian countries with Helen Richardson in 1926 and is notable as being the first work to rely on the private diary Dreiser kept during his months abroad, a part of which time was devoted ostensibly to discovering source material for the final Cowperwood novel, *The Stoic.*

Investigation into Dreiser's sources for fiction has been (and to an extent remains) a neglected field of criticism. Work in that fruitful area was undertaken by Philip Gerber in a series of essays delving into the research done by Dreiser preparatory to writing *The Financier, The Titan,* and *The Stoic.* These culminated in the first single-volume printing of these novels in *A Trilogy of Desire* (1972), introduced by Gerber, and in an extensive contribution to *Literary Monographs* 7 (1975). Intended as the concluding portion of a projected volume devoted to Dreiser's basis in fact for the Cowperwood trilogy, "Dreiser's *Stoic:* A Study in Literary Frustration" details the novelist's 30-year struggle to complete the Cowperwood story, which ended with Dreiser's death in 1945 and left his nearly finished manuscript to be concluded from notes and drafts by his widow, Helen Dreiser.

Under the editorship of Jack Salzman, *Modern Fiction Studies* in Autumn 1977 devoted a special issue to essays by Dreiser scholars such as Robert Forrey, Lester H. Cohen, Max Westbrook, and Frederic E. Rusch. A variety of Dreiser's novels were dealt with, including *The Financier* and *The Titan* (John O'Neill), *The "Genius"* (Dorothy Klopf), and *An American Tragedy* (Paul A. Orlov). Thomas P. Riggio wrote of the seldom-studied *A Traveler at Forty,* and Guy Szuberla presented an in-depth examination of Dreiser's fateful visit to the Chicago World's Fair in 1893. Of special note was an examination of *Sister Carrie* by Cathy N. and Arnold E. Davidson. Their essay, "Carrie's Sisters: The Popular Prototypes for Dreiser's Heroines," probed a neglected and almost unknown field, the popular "working girl" novels prevalent in the late nineteenth century. It offered a provocative and wholly convincing argument for the idea that Dreiser had these formula novels in mind as he composed *Sister Carrie.* Dreiser's own novel, say the Davidsons, is no less than a turning upside down of every known stereotype concerning the innocent maiden from the sticks whose virtue is threatened in the big city; they argue that it is in fact a parody of novels by Charlotte M. Brame, Bertha M. Clay, and other best-selling practitioners of these unrealistic romances. In so doing, the authors take Dreiser another step forward in the recognition of his artistry, crediting him with a skill not appreciated by those readers who in 1900 had been outraged by his portrait of a "sinning" but unrepentant and unpunished working girl.

The Davidsons' contribution picks up on a ground-breaking essay by Sybil B. Weir in *Pacific Coast Philology* (April 1972), which represents the beginnings of feminist criticism of Dreiser's fiction. Weir's "The Image of Women in Dreiser's Fiction, 1900-1925" opens with a candid presentation of the question:

> Dreiser is the first, and perhaps the only, major American novelist who refuses to present women only as symbols of the American ideal. His female characters may represent the American possibilities, but these possibilities are not, as 19th century fiction asserted, only pastoral and Edenic, nor, as 20th century fiction asserts, destructive and immoral. Unlike most American novelists, Dreiser accepts the aspirations of his heroines. Why shouldn't there be a female version of Horatio Alger? Why should women be expected to be inherently moral, disdainful of materialistic motives, presented as monsters if they are ambitious?[12]

Weir then takes up in turn Dreiser's major heroines – Carrie Meeber, Jennie Gerhardt, Aileen Butler Cowperwood, Angela Blue,

Roberta Alden, and Sondra Finchley – and persuasively presses her thesis, demonstrating the ways in which characteristically American attitudes toward sexuality stem from the capitalistic ethic and defending the stance taken by Dreiser that a sexual career does not automatically invalidate a woman's moral nature. Many writers prior to Weir had commented on Dreiser's inherently sympathetic attitude toward women in the modern era, but none had concentrated on that aspect of his work. In so doing, Weir points the way toward the future of Dreiser studies.

Chapter Ten

Dreiser Studies Flourish: The 1980s

[Dreiser] was the most American of novelists . . . and for a time he *was* American literature, the only writer worth talking about in the same breath with the European masters.
                                        – Richard Lingeman, 1990

The decade just past was a fruitful one for Dreiser studies. It opened auspiciously with the University of Pennsylvania Press edition of *Sister Carrie.* Representing the combined efforts of editors John C. Berkey, Alice M. Winters, James L. W. West III, and Neda Westlake, the "new" *Sister Carrie* attempts to establish the most acceptable text for the novel, which originally was worked on and revised not only by Dreiser himself but also by his wife Sara White Dreiser and his friend Arthur Henry. To identify the text Dreiser himself would have approved if free of outside influences was no easy task, and to reach this point the editors went back to the original manuscript (which Dreiser gave to his friend H. L. Mencken, who in turn donated it to the New York Public Library). This manuscript was read against the first edition for accuracy, and all cuts and emendations were studied in order to determine the hands that had written them and the closeness with which they hewed to what was perceived to have been Dreiser's intention. The result is a novel whose text differs considerably from that printed by Doubleday in 1900. The editors make it clear, however, that the Pennsylvania text cannot be considered "definitive" – and indeed that a truly definitive text for the novel can never be achieved.

The most significant change – and the most controversial – from the first edition was the elimination of the coda from the final chapter, those pages in which Carrie's state is summarized as she sits alone in her rocking chair in her hotel suite thinking herself lifted above "the tangle of human life," possessed of much that she had desired, yet waiting still – and in vain – for fulfillment, that happiness she had envisioned when she set out on her journey. In its new text the novel ends with Hurstwood's suicide, as he stretches himself out on his flophouse bed, turns on the gas jets, and thinks that final, hopeless thought: "What's the use?" Believing that Dreiser wished his novel to end on this note, where he originally brought it to a close, the editors have chosen not to allow the text to go further. Not all readers have agreed with this decision. When the book was first published, more than one reviewer made the point that the portrait of Hurstwood, the failure, had increasingly become Dreiser's focal point and that the depiction of his fall was the most affecting portion of the novel. The new edition lends strength to this view and the editors make the point that the ending usually printed was an addition made by Dreiser as a result of pressures placed on him by those helping him with his manuscript. What is lost – that final emphasis on the title character – is regretted by as many as might prefer the "new" ending.

The Pennsylvania *Sister Carrie* presents the student and scholar with most of the apparatus anyone might need for studying the history of the novel. In addition to restoring a multitude of passages cut from the original manuscript and supplying the actual names of places and persons that were altered at the publisher's insistence, the Pennsylvania *Carrie* supplies an extensive narrative history of the composition of the novel, useful period maps of Chicago and New York with relevant locations identified, and a collection of photographs picturing such places as the Casino Theatre and Sherry's Restaurant, which play roles in Carrie's story. This edition set a standard for future efforts at presenting authoritative texts of Dreiser's works.

The Pennsylvania edition was followed in 1985 by James L. W. West III's remarkable *A Sister Carrie Portfolio*, a large-format volume that focuses on the difficulties Dreiser faced in preparing and publishing his first novel. It supplies a "visual dimension" to the making of *Sister Carrie* by supplying facsimiles of the manuscript as well as pages of the texts and photographs of important historical documents used in preparing the new edition. Here a reader can see examples of the revisions Sara White Dreiser made in the manuscript

and typescript, cuts made by Arthur Henry, and corruptions introduced by typists and compositors as well as by in-house editors at
Doubleday. Photographs of many of the real persons and places
named in the manuscript as well as important letters that passed
between Dreiser, Arthur Henry, and Doubleday are included. The
work is an important supplement for anyone interested in *Sister
Carrie* and its history.

As one might expect, given the momentum behind the decade, a
multitude of books appeared, of a richer variety perhaps than in any
previous 10-year period. Each was valuable and each, in its own way,
added considerably to the swelling pool of facts and ideas concerning Dreiser.

One important example is the provocative reading of Dreiser's
major work provided by Lawrence E. Hussman, Jr., in *Dreiser and
His Fiction* (1983). Hussman's thesis links with the take/give,
me/we, self-seeking/group-welfare split in American society, an
internal tension he sees as characterizing Dreiser's fiction from start
to finish. As a pair, *Sister Carrie* and *Jennie Gerhardt* are seen as
exemplifying that dichotomy, and *The "Genius"* is seen as culminat-
ing in a tug-of-war between a desire to believe in Christian Science
and a conviction that the world is ruled by "a devil." Unlike the
usual critic, Hussman deals with Dreiser's short fiction, in which he
sees the same take/give conflict as being important. The strain
between desire and duty characterizes *An American Tragedy* as well,
but it is in *The Bulwark* and *The Stoic* that Hussman sees this theme
reaching its strongest expression as Dreiser apparently undergoes a
sort of conversion away from a belief in self-interest and toward a
belief in the primacy of service to society. This study is well argued,
well written, and valuable for its insights, whether or not a reader
ultimately agrees with the Hussman point of view.

A unique study, one that was badly needed, is Craig Brandon's
Murder in the Adirondacks (1986), an exhaustive examination of the
facts concerning the Gillette-Brown murder case on which *An American Tragedy* was based. Quite appropriately a newspaperman
himself, Brandon became fascinated with the case, which was heavily
reported in the newspapers, and spent five years poring over thou-
sands of pages of court transcripts and press accounts and in seeking
out local informants, including a good many relatives of persons who
had attended the Gillette trial or were otherwise involved in the case

and who left scrapbooks, letters, and other documents. The result is that we now have authentic and considerably expanded portraits of the principals in the case, as well as Grace Brown's love letters to Chester Gillette, the day-by-day log of their tragic trip to Big Moose Lake, a full depiction of the arrest and subsequent trial of Gillette, the poignant real-life role played in it by Chester's mother, and the eventual execution.

Besides constituting an exciting tale in its own right, the chief value of Brandon's book to Dreiser scholars may well be to confirm the manner in which the novelist deliberately distanced himself from his sources. Brandon makes clear the minimal research done by Dreiser and Helen Richardson on their 1923 trip through the New York area that was setting both for the case and for his novel. Dreiser was interested chiefly in pinning down the exact, yet broad, outlines of the story rather than adhering slavishly to fact. Thus he had no qualms, for instance, about playing with the geography of the various real-life sites, moving locales into closer proximity as it suited his artistic purpose. It is an amazing thing to see how very close Dreiser hewed to the outlines of the actual story while still preserving his artistic freedom to change, adapt, add, winnow, and invent for his own purposes. The implications for Dreiser's stature as an artist are large and the claims for the novel as a work of art considerably greater than any of Dreiser's detractors might wish to acknowledge. Brandon's is a significant document; it should inspire further investigation into Dreiser's use of sources for his fiction.

Among the best studies of Dreiser's artistry is that offered by Philip Fisher in *Hard Facts* (1985). It deals with three American novelists whose "transforming power" enabled them to establish enduring works that caught the central truths of the times in which they lived. For these three – James Fenimore Cooper, Harriet Beecher Stowe, and Dreiser – Fisher employs the word "ordinary," by which he intends to establish their command of "the universality of the everyday. . . . that which is central and accurate."[1] The "hard facts" of the title are three indelible events of American social history: the killing of a man (specifically of the Indian), for which Cooper invented the wilderness as his archetypal setting; the moral outrage of slavery, for which Stowe went to the family farm or plantation; and finally the "severe evacuation and objectification of the self that followed from the economic and future-oriented world of capitalism," for which Dreiser turned to the new industrial city, the arena of the street. According to Fisher, Dreiser created this setting in *Sister Carrie* and carried it forward through his work to its culmination in *An American Tragedy*.

In the capitalistic city all things are purchasable. Carrie Meeber, as an actress, is a commodity to be packaged and advertised and delivered, bought and sold. Desire is the motivation; the thinking process is displaced by shopping for what is desired. Fisher follows this thesis through the *Tragedy*, demonstrating the manner in which Clyde Griffiths and Roberta Alden "shop" for an abortion, passing through a variety of mercantile offices – clothing store, drug store, physician's office – in their fruitless search for the commodity they desire above all. Buildings and streets become primary symbols as Fisher emphasizes the centrality of such places as the Green-Davidson Hotel and the Casino Theatre as "terminal points of desire" (Fisher, 131). "Work" is transformed into "acting," and Carrie Meeber's choice of profession underscores this momentous change in American values. The self is swathed in clothes, then in buildings (Fisher points out Dreiser's choice of a factory that makes collars as Clyde's chosen job location). Clyde's wages are poured into clothes, creating the visible self by which he wishes to be identified, and among the decisive clues condemning him at his trial are his pair of straw hats, his clothing, and his suitcase. Fisher's arguments are brilliantly conceived, lucidly stated, and persuasively illustrated. His study marks an important step forward in our perception of Dreiser as an artist capable of considerable insight and subtlety.

Because of his stature as a novelist, Dreiser's work in shorter forms has been largely ignored, even though, paradoxically, it is through his short stories, as printed in anthologies, that he is usually introduced to the student. Joseph Griffin's *The Small Canvas* (1985) is the first book to be devoted wholly to the short fiction. The 11 stories that were collected in *Free, and Other Stories* are analyzed, as well as the 15 that made up *Chains*, and 5 uncollected in book form. There is much to be gained from Griffin's study, including an augmented appreciation of Dreiser's artistry in stories such as "Sanctuary" and "Typhoon," whose aptness of imagery is stressed. Most important, Griffin demonstrates that Dreiser was a considerably better short-story craftsman than critics have generally credited him with being, notwithstanding the fact that his true strength is to be found in his novels, those "large canvases" that allowed room for his accretive method of writing.

In *From Fact to Fiction* (1985) Shelley Fisher Fishkin establishes Dreiser within the context of significant American writers who began their writing careers as journalists: Walt Whitman, Mark Twain, Ernest Hemingway, and John Dos Passos. These writers (as well as others, such as Sinclair Lewis and Willa Cather) served as apprentices on newspapers and magazines before making their individual breakouts into imaginative writing, usually then selecting the novel as their genre. Working in journalism on a daily basis, says Fishkin, exposed these writers to the breadth and diversity of experience existing in the "real world" around them, supplying them with topics, ideas, and incidents that would emerge as important elements in their later works. Working at their craft under the supervision of experienced editors and writing against strict deadlines, they learned to become precise observers of the fascinating diversity of American life that met the eye on every city street and lane. They were required to pay attention to the difference between fact and conjecture and, via the editorial blue pencil, they took lessons in writing that would lead toward their characteristic styles as mature writers.

Dreiser's prose style, which even Fishkin finds too often "turgid and expansive," is easily traced back to his journalistic beginnings. So is his intricate understanding of the way in which American society is organized and operates, as well as his comprehension of the limited and often distorted picture of that society that was allowed into the pages of the daily newspapers during the 1890s. One senses that Dreiser's writing instincts necessarily had been straitjacketed by the ultraconservative policies of timid editors who, for instance, would not allow any negative criticism of the powerful steel magnates in a city such as Pittsburgh. Unhappiness with this situation played a considerable role in impelling Dreiser toward a new start, one in which he might feel considerably more his own master. Fishkin identifies the Chicago columnist Eugene Field, whose daily observations Dreiser read avidly, as a specific source for a number of stylistic traits that later marred Dreiser's prose: "inflated, high-sounding diction," sometimes grotesquely misused, inverted phraseology such as "glances arch," and a misguided preference for the latinate expression where the native English idiom might better serve his purpose.[2]

Studies such as Fishkin's are valuable also in making clear the powerful influence on Dreiser of the American city and its characteristic events, which impressed him with tendencies that later provided a core of subject matter for fiction. It was as a newspaperman, for instance, that Dreiser first became intimately acquainted with the vast and growing gulf between rich and the poor on a national scale, and his experience with urban business and political realities taught him how and why that widening gulf would not easily be closed. From such investigations came his Cowperwood trilogy, which, as Fishkin points out, is based closely on factual reports published in Chicago and New York newspapers. In *Sister Carrie* Dreiser had achieved verisimilitude by incorporating actual newspaper items, especially advertisements, directly into his manuscript, and his *An American Tragedy* makes extensive use of the stories published in the New York *World.*

Much of the evidence for Fishkin's conclusions concerning the influence of his newspaper days on Dreiser's writing style and his choice of subjects and themes for fiction is now directly available to students, thanks to T. D. Nostwich, who has edited two volumes of Dreiser's early contributions to Chicago and other midwestern papers. In *Theodore Dreiser: Journalism* and *Theodore Dreiser's "Heard in the Corridors,"* both published in 1988, Nostwich reminds us that the newspaper stories he reprints comprise no more than a slight fraction of the novelist's writing published between 1892 and 1895. The full record of Dreiser's newspaper stories would make a work exceeding 2,300 pages. During these apprentice years all of urban America from Chicago's Auditorium Theatre to Pittsburgh's Schenley Park, from the morgue to Potter's Field, became Dreiser's private turf. No writer surpassed him in portraying the city dwellers of the gilded era, be they millionaires or ragpickers.

From these early columns much can be learned about Dreiser's own character and biography, including his strangely superstitious nature, which came close to an outright belief in clairvoyance. Perhaps the most pertinent of all these "biographical" pieces are those written in 1893 for the *Saint Louis Democrat* detailing Dreiser's assignment to accompany a railroad car of Missouri schoolmarms to the World's Columbian Exposition in Chicago. This trip, relatively unexamined until recently, was a most significant one, for among the teachers in his charge was "Miss White" – the future

Mrs. Dreiser. Dreiser's increasing infatuation with the redheaded
Miss White becomes clear in the feature stories he wired back from
the great World's Fair. And there are strong hints that, in escorting
his new friend through the central portion of Chicago where the
skyscraper was being born, through intimidating canyons of brick
and stone, an area abuzz with mercantile activity, Dreiser may have
come to the idea for what in a half-dozen years would be the
opening scene of *Sister Carrie*, in which a "peach" of a girl, small-
town bred, meets an interesting young man on a railroad train
coming into Chicago and then is turned loose to fend for herself
amid the welter of an industrial city on the make.

Other experiences capable of being mined for *Sister Carrie*
abound, some of them suggesting the fate of George Hurstwood. As
Dreiser stopped over in Toledo, working his way toward the mecca
of New York, he was a close observer of a great strike of workers on
the Toledo Electric Street Railroad. He covered the strike for the
Toledo Blade. At the local traction company's office he watched
while applicants eager to replace the strikers were hired and then
sent out on perilous journeys through streets lined by angry workers
and their sympathizers. Dreiser rode on such a car, operated by its
new and frightened conductor, while a jeering crowd shouted
"Scab!" and threw corn and beans. Before the run was over, the new
conductor had been struck by heavy mud balls. In this experience,
one can easily perceive the inspiration for the story of a desperate
Hurstwood accepting employment during the Brooklyn transit strike
and having a similar nerve-rattling and physically dangerous trip,
severe enough to shake his confidence and his health. Other journalistic pieces suggest Hurstwood also. "Did He Blow Out the Gas?"
written in New York in 1895, is Dreiser's report on a shabbily
dressed man who registered at the Bryant Park Hotel and was found
dead the next morning, with the gas jets open but unlighted.

In the standoff between rich and poor, powerful and impotent,
Dreiser's sympathies invariably went with the underdog, a position
that would mark the entire range of his fiction – and his life. Particularly in Pittsburgh, he attempted to give voice to his concern over
the concentration of wealth and power to the detriment of the
masses. In "Fenced Off the Earth" he addressed the plight of 40
families walled off into a metropolitan isolation in which no one, not
even the iceman on his daily rounds, can reach them, because the

all-powerful Baltimore and Ohio Railroad has them firmly under its lion's paw. Having decided it wants the street fronting their property, the B & O has magisterially constructed there a high wooden fence and topped it with a "barbed wire crown" that prevents both entry and exit. While the families protest in vain and a corrupted city hall delays the essential injunction that might prevent this trespass, the railroad, comments Dreiser, "says nothing but saws more wood for its fence." In these experiences and many similar ones, a reader can see why Dreiser might have been impelled to write a trilogy of novels detailing the arrogance of monopolistic power in the land of the free.

Nostwich's *Theodore Dreiser: Journalism* (announced as being the first of two such collections) appeared as a portion of the most significant Dreiser publishing venture in the 1980s, a projected complete edition of Dreiser's works undertaken by the University of Pennsylvania Press. The revised *Sister Carrie* of 1981 had been the first volume in the edition, but the publication of Dreiser's "complete works" received a significant impetus through the formation in 1986 of an editorial board empowered to superintend the edition, with Thomas P. Riggio of the University of Connecticut as editor-in-chief and Arthur Cascioto, Philip Gerber, T. D. Nostwich, Noel Polk, James L. W. West III, and Neda M. Westlake as board members, joined by Daniel H. Traister of the University of Pennsylvania Library Special Collections. The ambitious aim of the complete Dreiser edition is to publish authoritative texts of all of Dreiser's published works as well as important works remaining unpublished at the time of the author's death and allied works bearing centrally on Dreiser's life and career.

Prominent among these allied works have been Thomas P. Riggio's editions of *American Diaries, (1902-1926)* (1982) and *Dreiser-Mencken Letters* (1987). *American Diaries* reveals Dreiser's powerful tendency toward hypochondria and provides details of the depressive abyss into which he tumbled after the publishing debacle of *Sister Carrie* in 1900. Dreiser's own words now allow one to share in the physical symptoms of the writer's malaise and understand some of the possible reasons for his long hiatus from fiction writing. This entry from 1902 is representative:

> Monday Dec. 8th Rose at seven having experienced a poor night. The usual wakefulness began at 12 M. with some slight head pains thereafter and a few

dreams. Rose at seven and went through usual routine, reading, dining and walking out a little with the result that I felt very tired by night. Indeed I felt very drowsy during the afternoon but did not lie down. Went to bed at nine feeling very weary but slept no later than twelve M, when I awoke and dozed fitfully until morning. My feeling during the day had been about the same as the day before. No marked head pains but some lassitude, no imaginative or initiative powers. Ate normally and with relish. (*Diaries*, 72)

Diaries Dreiser kept during his residence in Greenwich Village in 1917 and 1918 record his efforts to keep up his writing following the great stress occasioned by censorship of *The "Genius"* but are most notable for his outspoken record of a variety of love affairs. Readers who may have thought Dreiser frank in depicting sexual encounters in his novels can now see how very circumspect, by comparison, those accounts had been.

"This day I met Helen" begins Dreiser's entry of 13 September 1919, in the diary recounting his love affair with Helen Richardson and the writing of *An American Tragedy*. That Helen, despite his many lovers, was the great and enduring love of Dreiser's life cannot be doubted. Struck by her poise, her natural intuition, her "ravishing smile" and "dazzling skin," her ability to project simultaneously adult sensuality and youthful innocence, Dreiser was smitten. The very day following her arrival at his door, he recorded that he had "spent this entire night thinking of Helen. Very restless. At 2 A.M. was about to call her up. In a perfect fever of desire." Helen reciprocated. "Sex satisfaction & agreement have brought us close together," confided Dreiser to his private pages. "She is satisfied with me & I with her. . . . My life seems torn up by the roots. Feel that I am due for a long period with her, maybe years" (*Diaries*, 278, 280, 282). Their sexual encounters are recorded in passages notable for their utter candor and infinite detail.

For the sake of Helen, Dreiser cut all of his New York connections and set off cross-country to Hollywood, where he wrote, although sporadically, and supported Helen in her bid for movie stardom. Returning to the East in 1923, he made his own record of his and Helen's trip to upstate New York in search of primary data concerning the Gillette-Brown murder that he had selected as the basis for his new novel. Late in June they started out, by automobile, for Cortland, Old Forge, and Big Moose Lake (the Big Bittern Lake of that novel). On 4 July he wrote: "Talk[ed] to the guide who found Grace Browns body. His recollections of Gillette & her" (*Diaries*, 401). They stopped also in Herkimer, where Chester Gillette had been tried and sentenced to death, making inquiries along the way of persons who might recollect details of the 1906 murder case that he could use in his story. Those who may have thought *An American Tragedy* derived wholly from newspaper accounts can now see for themselves that Dreiser went considerably further as he prepared to write his masterwork.

Different in kind but of equal value in revealing aspects of Dreiser's life and career, *Dreiser-Mencken Letters*, also edited by Riggio, is a work of inestimable aid to the student. H. L. Mencken was not only Dreiser's first important literary defender but also his closest and most influential friend throughout his career. They had their differences, as any individualistic and volatile personalities are likely to have, and at times, sometimes for years, they swore off each other, only to reconcile and in the end remain each other's greatest admirers. Late in their careers they began giving serious consideration to the manner in which posterity might view them, both separately and as a "team," and they took steps that would ensure access to vital documents for scholars in the future. As the letters collected by Riggio make clear, this concerted action began with Dreiser's informing Mencken that the University of Pennsylvania was "taking over all [his] stuff, lock, stock, & barrel," including "a lot" of Mencken's letters. Dreiser wished to know whether his old friend wanted these to go to Philadelphia.

As it turned out, Mencken himself had begun to collect copies of his letters as aids in the writing of a memoir and was delighted to discover that his correspondence with Dreiser had not been tossed into the trash bin. His own archives contained hundreds of letters from Dreiser. Joined, would not these sets of letters complement each other as the twin halves of a most interesting record? They would not be brought together for another 40 years, but now, thanks to Riggio, a student of Dreiser and/or Mencken, or of the age which in one sense they came to dominate, has at hand as complete a record as can ever hope to be established of their confidential words to each other as well as behind-the-scenes accounts of the many literary battles – including that against censorship – in which they played leading roles during the first half of the century. In 1,200 letters the two men record the days of fierce battles, especially those prior to 1920 when they fought happily side by side in the literary trenches, determined to make the ghosts of the Puritans gibber in the streets.

The bonds that held them together were based on mutual appreciation. In his most direct expression of those bonds, Dreiser wrote of his perception that he would never have been able to make a dent with his novels had not Mencken fought for him valiantly, unstintingly, and even murderously: "I remember how, almost fatalistically, you arrived in my life when, from a literary point of view, I was down and out, and you proceeded to fight for me. Night and day apparently. Swack! Smack! Crack! Until finally you succeeded in chasing an entire nation of literary flies to cover. It was lovely! It was classic."[3] Mencken was even more succinct, saying that Dreiser was the only American writer whose novels were suitable reading for civilized people. Whatever else changed, these attitudes endured, and the record is now there for all to see.

One of the hitherto obscure chapters in Dreiser's life documented in *American Diaries* – the writer's psychoneurotic plunge following *Sister Carrie* – is treated further in another volume in the Pennsylvania edition, Richard W. Dowell's edition of *An Amateur Laborer* (1983). One of the numerous manuscripts that Dreiser never completed or published, *An Amateur Laborer* is the record of those terrible years when "thought failed me, reason failed me," and he feared that it might all be over for him. His weight (at six feet of height) plummeted to 140 pounds, then to 130: "Coupled with this my nervous system grew weaker and I was now subject to the most distressing hallucinations. [At night] I would jump up and look about me, terrified and cold with sweat" (*Laborer*, 25). As therapy, Dreiser enrolled in the health camp run by William Muldoon and then undertook physical work as a day laborer on the New York Central Railroad. His account is unfinished, but the chapters that were preserved reveal the jeopardy to his life and career.

As concerns biography, the big event of the decade was the publication in 1986 of Richard Lingeman's *Theodore Dreiser: At the Gates of the City 1871-1907*. The first of a projected two-volume biography, Lingeman's study carries Dreiser from the time of his birth until the time of *Sister Carrie*'s "rebirth" in a new edition published by B. W. Dodge. Building on the work done by Dorothy

Dudley, Robert Elias, and W. A. Swanberg, Lingeman draws on much new material that had been discovered or been made available over the decades. As a result, he has been able to place a new emphasis on the novelist's father, John Paul Dreiser, correcting somewhat the biased view given by his jaundiced son and filling out the hitherto incomplete record. This work is important in Dreiser studies, for Dreiser's German father sailed to America from a non-English-speaking nation, and as a consequence his immigrant experience was that of the complete outsider. The fact of the Dreisers' "difference" is crucial to understanding Theodore's stance vis-à-vis society and the early development of a defensive attitude that is reflected accurately in the subtitle of Lingeman's book.

In the years since Swanberg wrote, Dreiser's erotic courtship letters to Sara Osborne White have been released from the tight restrictions that at one time discouraged their use, and Lingeman draws on them at considerable length in order to expand his portrait of Dreiser at a most critical juncture in his young manhood: his marriage. Lingeman does well in presenting an American context of historical, social, and economic details within which the novelist's life proceeds. He brings into sharp focus the influence of sexuality, saying early on that erotic energy was what powered Dreiser's creative force. That concept becomes a controlling device in Lingeman's analysis of *Sister Carrie*, with its turnabout image of Carrie seducing her pair of would-be seducers from the stage of the theater in which they watch adoringly as she plays Laura in "Under the Gaslight." Lingeman suggests that the fictional Carrie achieved a reality that made her a genuine rival to Dreiser's bride of two years, although Sara Dreiser was not quite perceptive enough to notice that her husband was "borne along by an erotic subcurrent of desire for his heroine."[4] The publication in 1990 of *Theodore Dreiser: An American Journey, 1908-1945* completed Lingeman's biography.

A most unusual book, and one for which Dreiser scholars are grateful, is Clara Jaeger's autobiographical *Philadelphia Rebel* (1988). The author was Clara Clark, daughter of a prominent family of Germantown, Pennsylvania, who on a hot summer afternoon in 1931 picked up Dreiser's just-published autobiography *Dawn* and became enamored of its author. She was drawn to Dreiser by his frank and honest admissions concerning himself, his awkward appearance, his openly admitted embarrassment and suffering, his longing for love and beauty, his dumbstruck wonder at the world. Before long, Clara Clark found herself writing to Dreiser; ultimately, she traveled to New York, becoming Dreiser's lover and then one of his secretaries while he labored to complete *The Stoic* during 1933 and 1934. This is a frank account, structured in terms of diary entries, and it provides valuable biographical data concerning a portion of Dreiser's life about which too little has been published. One is grateful that Jaeger, before it was too late, has made certain that her story is accessible.

In 1981 Donald Pizer's *Critical Essays on Theodore Dreiser* brought together 37 significant essays, including a group that had appeared in *The Stature of Theodore Dreiser* but adding a number of those written during the nearly thirty years that had intervened. These included Roger Asselineau's unusual study "Theodore Dreiser's Transcendentalism" (1961), William L. Phillips's discerning essay "The Imagery of Dreiser's Novels" (1963), as well as Pizer's "American Literary Naturalism: The Example of Dreiser" (1977).

Efforts at making accessible long-out-of-print works by Dreiser himself have been continued by the Japanese-born scholar Yoshinobu Hakutani in his two-volume collection *Selected Magazine Articles of Theodore Dreiser* (1985 and 1987). Hakutani points out that between 1897 and the publication of *Sister Carrie* in 1900 Dreiser was busily engaged in free-lancing for a variety of magazines. At least 120 articles appeared, 28 of which are collected in Hakutani's first volume. They represent a wide spectrum of American life, from interviews and investigations that would surface later in Dreiser's fiction – studies of Philip D. Armour and Marshall Field, the Chicago nabobs, and of metropolitan New York breadlines – to reports on contemporary painters, photographers, and sculptors. Twenty-six additional articles, representing something of the same variety, are gathered into Hakutani's second volume. At the very beginning of the decade, Hakutani had published *Young Dreiser* (1980), a critical study that concentrated on Dreiser's youth and his writing apprenticeship and subsequent free-lance career up to the time of *Sister Carrie*. Hakutani's fascination with Dreiser, beginning in his native Japan, and his subsequent, continuing contributions to Dreiser studies are indicative of the impact Dreiser's efforts have made on cultures abroad.

Voices from India reflect the persistent appeal of Dreiser there. Early in 1984 L. Jeganatha Raja devoted a special issue of his journal *Life, Art and Literature* to Dreiser studies, and later that year he published an expansion of that issue as *Theodore Dreiser: The Man and His Message*. Contributors included the American scholars Richard Dowell, Vera Dreiser, Philip Gerber, Donald Goodyear, the Japanese-born Yoshinobu Hakutani, as well as a group of Indian writers: P. Marudanayagam, R. N. Mookerjee, Brij Mohan Singh, and Raja himself. Another Indian scholar, now working in Canada, Arun Mukherjee published *The Gospel of Wealth in the American Novel* in 1987. Devoted largely to Dreiser, Mukherjee's volume expresses an appreciation of Dreiser as one of the few American (or world) writers given to placing characters within a specific social nexus and then exploring their socialization. She takes as her theme the literary reaction to the capitalistic system, with its inherent inequities, concentrating on "the way American novelists respond rhetorically to the discourse of the American businessman and his apologists."[5] Of interest to her are those writers who allow themselves to be co-opted by the system as well as those, such as Dreiser, who have worked subversively to undermine it. Mukherjee brilliantly outlines the way in which the raw Darwinism of laissez-faire capitalism was transformed into a glorified "romance of business" during the late nineteenth century; and she explains how the profit motive was turned by adherents into a glorious and even heroic adventure, "a new test of manliness" in which questions of ethics and morality could be conveniently brushed aside. *Sister Carrie*, argues Mukherjee, is no less than a parody of popular notions concerning commerce, a novel whose dominant tone is ironic.

A happy note was sounded in 1990 when *The Heath Anthology of American Literature* appeared, Dreiser being represented not by what had become the standard offerings, "The Second Choice" or "Free," but by a new and authoritative edition of the seldom-reprinted "Typhoon," prepared by Dreiser textual editor James Hutchisson.

Among things that Dreiser's readers can look forward to include a special Dreiser issue of *Papers on Language and Literature* edited by James L. W. West III. It will include unusual items such as an examination of the diary kept by Dreiser during his 1927 visit to the

Soviet Union, an analysis of the novelist's handwriting, a review of
the essay contest held by Boni and Liveright subsequent to the
publication of *An American Tragedy,* a new biographical
consideration of Dreiser's final years, and the first publication of
surviving chapters of Dreiser's unfinished novel *The "Rake."*
Scholars scheduled for contributions include Arthur Casciato, Robert
Coltrane, Rose Gatti, Philip Gerber, James Hutchisson, Robert Myers,
Katherine Plank, Thomas Riggio, and Frederic Rusch.

The Pennsylvania edition of Theodore Dreiser expects to
continue issuing authoritative texts of Dreiser's books; the next
offering is T. D. Nostwich's edition of *Newspaper Days,* based on the
complete manuscript preserved in the Dreiser Collection. The new
edition will reinstate a large body of material deleted on first publication, giving readers a considerably expanded and corrected idea of
Dreiser's journalistic apprenticeship. *Newspaper Days* is to be
followed by *Jennie Gerhardt, The Financier, Dawn, Twelve Men,*
and other volumes.

In 1990 a conference organized by Philip Gerber was held at
Brockport, New York, observing the ninetieth year of publication of
Sister Carrie and the sixty-fifth year of *An American Tragedy.* A
number of the newer approaches to Dreiser and his fiction were
evident in presentations by James L. W. West, III, on the editing of
Sister Carrie and *Jennie Gerhardt;* by Nancy Barrineau, on the rela-
tionship of Dreiser's novels to popular "working girl" novels of the
nineteenth century; and by Leonard Cassuto, on the interpretation of
Dreiser's fiction according to principles set down by psychoanalyst
Jacques Lacan. Of special interest were a treatment of the state of
Dreiser studies in India by Arun Mukherjee and a proposal for the
significance of *Sister Carrie* to African-American readers by Earleen
De La Perriere.[6]

New approaches to Dreiser were in evidence also at the 1991
conference of the American Literature Association, where Leonard
Cassuto continued his Lacanian interpretation, this time as applied
to *The Financier,* and German-born Irene Gammel presented a feminist reading of Dreiser's treatment of female sexuality. The formation
of an international Dreiser Society took an important step forward in
a meeting conducted by Miriam Gogol and Frederic Rusch and
attended by a roomful of Dreiser scholars from various sections of
the United States as well as from India and Japan.

scholars will continue to pursue lines of investigation now in an embryonic state and that certain of these directions display considerable promise: the questions of Dreiser's artistry, the importance of his writing to issues concerning women, and the new light to be shed by psychoanalytic criticism. In addition, more scholarly voices from abroad can be expected to augment the continuing, indeed accelerating, interest in Dreiser on a global scale.

Note: Since this volume was composed, a number of important publications concerning Dreiser, then tentative, have come into print. These include the special number of *Papers on Language and Literature,* T. D. Nostwich's restored edition of *Newspaper Days,* and the second and final volume of Richard Lingeman's biography. The Pizer, Dowell, Rusch bibliography has been updated to include the nearly 20 years of Dreiser scholarship occurring since 1975. Donald Pizer has edited *New Essays on Sister Carrie. Jennie Gerhardt* has been slated for publication in the Pennsylvania Edition of Theodore Dreiser. And a new Dreiser scholar, Laura Hapke, has reaffirmed Dreiser's leadership in the literature of social consciousness in her study *Tales of the Working Girl.* Where relevant, these works are included in the Selected Bibliography.

Notes and References

Chapter One

1. For factual information up to "Newspaper Days," I have relied heavily on Dreiser's autobiography *Dawn*, which documents these early years extensively, although not with invariable reliability.

2. Shortened later to Snepp; as such, referred to in Dreiser's autobiographical writings.

3. For documentation of Dreiser's sexual activity, see his *American Diaries 1902-1926*, ed. Thomas P. Riggio (Philadelphia: University of Pennsylvania Press, 1982); hereafter cited in text as *Diaries*.

4. *Dawn* (New York: Horace Liveright, 1931), 200; hereafter cited in text.

5. For material from this point to the end of the chapter, I have relied heavily on Dreiser's autobiography *A Book about Myself* (later called *Newspaper Days*).

6. *A Book about Myself* (New York: Boni & Liveright, 1922), 132-33; hereafter cited in text as *Myself*.

7. C. T. Yerkes was used later as the prototype for Frank Cowperwood in *The Financier* (1912).

8. This story appears under the title "McEwen of the Shining Slave Makers" in *Free, and Other Stories* (New York: Boni & Liveright, 1918); hereafter cited in the text as *Free*.

9. These stories appear in *Free, and Other Stories*, the first under the title "Old Roagum and His Theresa."

10. Incredible as it may seem, Dreiser insisted that this was the process by which the novel came to be written – title first and story later. It seems probable, however, that his own sisters' experiences had long been in his mind as potential literary material and that it was this "sister" connection that conjured up the title as he began to think about a novel.

Chapter Two

1. Citations concerning the story are from *Sister Carrie* (New York: Doubleday, Page & Co., 1900); hereafter cited in text as *Carrie*.

2. *The Color of a Great City* (New York: Boni & Liveright, 1923), 99.

3. *A Hoosier Holiday* (New York: John Lane Co., 1916), 253.

Chapter Three

1. William Dean Howells, *Criticism and Fiction* (New York: Harpers, 1959), 70. Some may consider my treatment of Howells unnecessarily harsh, but he pursued realism for only a short distance. His refusal to lend his immense prestige to the defense of Dreiser when *The "Genius"* came under fire is indicative of his later, more conservative stance.

2. Frank Luther Mott's *Golden Multitudes* reports the best-sellers of the era as including the Reverend Wright's *Shepherd of the Hills* (1907) and *The Winning of Barbara Worth* (1911) along with Porter's *Freckles* (1903) and *The Girl of the Limberlost* (1909).

3. Robert H. Elias, ed., *Letters of Theodore Dreiser* (Philadelphia: University of Pennsylvania Press, 1959), 3:980; hereafter cited in text.

4. This period in Dreiser's life is reflected in "Culhane, the Solid Man," one of the portraits in *Twelve Men* (New York: Boni & Liveright, 1919) and is documented by Dreiser in his *An Amateur Laborer* (Philadelphia: University of Pennsylvania Press, 1983); hereafter cited in text as *Laborer*.

5. *Jennie Gerhardt* (New York: Harper & Brothers, 1911), 10; hereafter cited in text as *Jennie*.

6. Dreiser refers to Jennie Gerhardt as "my pet heroine" in *A Hoosier Holiday* when commenting on the similarity of Erie, Pennsylvania, to Jennie's native city of Columbus, Ohio, a city Dreiser had never visited at the time he used it as the setting for his novel. The author's affection for Jennie is evident at once in practically every reference he makes to her or to the novel; it was an affection that was contagious, H. L. Mencken being among those who were swept up by Jennie's story.

Chapter Four

1. *Hey, Rub-a-Dub-Dub!* (New York: Boni & Liveright, 1920), 74; hereafter cited in text as *Hey*.

2. Ellen Moers, *Two Dreisers* (New York: Viking, 1969), xii.

3. Stuart P. Sherman, "The Barbaric Naturalism of Mr. Dreiser," in *The Stature of Theodore Dreiser*, ed. Alfred Kazin and Charles Shapiro (Bloomington: Indiana University Press, 1955), 78; hereafter cited in text.

4. This and related statements are to be found in "Equation Inevitable," a central essay in *Hey, Rub-A-Dub-Dub!*, 157-81.

5. *The Financier* (New York: Harper & Brothers, 1912), 47; hereafter cited in text as *Financier*.

6. Edwin Lefevre, "What Availeth It?" *Everybody's Magazine* 24 (June 1911): 836-48; hereafer cited in text.

7. Charles E. Russell, "Where Did You Get It, Gentlemen?" *Everybody's Magazine* 17 (September 1907): 348-60.

8. *The Titan* (New York: New York, 1914), 125.

9. Sherman's article, "The Barbaric Naturalism of Mr. Dreiser," already cited, is worth reading in its entirety as an example of the extreme right-wing reaction to Dreiser's novels in the early part of the century.

10. *The Stoic* (New York: Doubleday, 1947), 283; hereafter cited in text as *Stoic.*

11. Robert H. Elias, *Theodore Dreiser: Apostle of Nature* (New York: Knopf, 1949), 160; hereafter cited in text.

Chapter Five

1. Helen Dreiser, *My Life with Dreiser* (Cleveland: World, 1951), 81.

2. *The "Genius"* (New York: John Lane Co., 1915), 12; hereafter cited in text as "Genius."

3. The description of this painting tallies rather precisely with the elements in Alfred Stieglitz's 1893 photograph *Winter, Fifth Avenue.* It is an instance of Dreiser's easiness in utilizing source materials. He admired Stieglitz's work immensely, as well as that of the verist painters, and he felt that in his novels he was attempting to convey the same impressions.

4. In the *Letters* (vol. 1) Suzanne Dale is revealed to be Thelma Cudlipp, and Dreiser's infatuation is manifest, even downright embarrassing, as he addresses her as "Flower Face" and "Honeypot."

5. Dorothy Dudley, *Forgotten Frontiers: Dreiser and the Land of the Free* (New York: Harrison Smith & Robert Haas, 1932), 335-36.

Chapter Six

1. My account of the writing of *An American Tragedy* is based largely on Helen Dreiser's recollections expressed in *My Life with Dreiser.*

2. For a full account of his Russian visit, see *Dreiser Looks at Russia* (New York: Boni & Liveright, 1928).

3. Mark Shorer, *Sinclair Lewis: An American Life* (New York: McGraw-Hill, 1961), 546-47.

4. Sinclair Lewis, "Our Formula for Fiction," in *The Stature of Theodore Dreiser,* 111-12.

5. Lewis was instrumental in seeing that the 1944 Award of Merit Medal of the National Institute of Arts and Letters was given to Dreiser. He wished his part in the matter to be kept secret, being afraid that Dreiser, should he discover the truth, might reject the medal.

Chapter Seven

1. Louise Campbell, ed., *Letters to Louise* (Philadelphia: University of Pennsylvania Press, 1959), 106-7.

2. A reader of Dreiser's autobiographies, works of nonfiction, and letters soon becomes acclimated to these outbursts, which frequently come

unheralded. Curiously, the more often they occur, the more one may be convinced of Dreiser's basically religious nature. Dreiser's suggestion that the word "organized" should preface the Marxist slogan "religion is the opium of the people" perhaps reveals more precisely the nature of his complaint concerning religion.

3. *The Bulwark* (Garden City, N.Y.: Doubleday, 1946), 12.

4. The best descriptions concerning the change in Dreiser's attitude regarding his father are found in *A Book about Myself,* particularly in chapter 39. Dreiser had been away from home for a year and now, visiting the World's Fair, he was able to see his father with greater objectivity.

Chapter Eight

1. Jack Salzman, ed., *Theodore Dreiser: The Critical Reception* (New York: Lewis, 1972), 3, 10, 11; hereafter cited in text.

2. Ernest A. Baker, *A Guide to the Best Fiction in English* (New York: Macmillan, 1913), 463.

3. H. L. Mencken, "The Dreiser Bugaboo," in *The Stature of Theodore Dreiser,* 84-91.

4. Randolph Bourne, "The Art of Theodore Dreiser," in *The History of a Literary Radical* (New York: S. A. Russell, 1956), 12.

5. Burton Rascoe, *Theodore Dreiser* (New York: McBride, 1925), 10.

6. Russell Blankenship, *American Literature as an Expression of the National Mind* (New York: Holt, 1931); hereafter cited in text.

7. Alfred Kazin, *On Native Grounds* (New York: Reynal & Hitchcock, 1942), 89.

Chapter Nine

1. Van Wyck Brooks, *The Confident Years: 1885-1915* (New York: Dutton, 1951), 305, 317.

2. F. O. Matthiessen, *Theodore Dreiser* (New York: William Sloane, 1951), 59-60, 233.

3. Maxwell Geismar, *Rebels and Ancestors: The American Novel, 1890-1915* (Boston: Houghton Mifflin, 1953), 302.

4. Kenneth S. Lynn, "Theodore Dreiser: The Man of Ice," in *The Dream of Success* (Boston: Little, Brown, 1955), 13-74.

5. Charles Child Walcutt, "Theodore Dreiser: The Wonder and Terror of Life," in *American Literary Naturalism, A Divided Stream* (Minneapolis: University of Minnesota Press, 1956).

6. Marguerite Tjader, *Theodore Dreiser: A New Dimension* (Norwalk, Conn.: Silvermine, 1965), 1-2.

7. Dust-jacket blurb on Moers's book.

8. Richard Poirier, *A World Elsewhere* (London: Chatte & Windus, 1967), vii-xi.

9. Robert Penn Warren, *Homage to Theodore Dreiser* (New York: Random House, 1971), 84.

10. Vera Dreiser, *My Uncle Theodore* (New York: Nash, 1976), 9.

11. Eugene O'Neill, *Strange Interlude* (New York: Boni & Liveright, 1928), 351.

12. Sybil B. Weir, "The Image of Women in Dreiser's Fiction, 1900-1925," *Pacific Coast Philology*, April 1972, 65.

Chapter Ten

1. Philip Fisher, "The Life History of Objects: The Naturalistic Novel and the City," in *Hard Facts* (New York: Oxford University Press, 1985), 8.

2. Shelley Fisher Fishkin, "Theodore Dreiser," in *From Fact to Fiction* (New York: Oxford University Press, 1985), 97, 98.

3. Thomas P. Riggio, ed., *Dreiser-Mencken Letters* (Philadelphia: University Press of Pennsylvania, 1987), 690-91.

4. Richard Lingeman, *Theodore Dreiser: At the Gates of the City, 1871-1907* (New York: G. P. Putnam's Sons, 1986), 251.

5. Arun Mukherjee, *The Gospel of Wealth in the American Novel* (Totowa, N.J.: Barnes & Noble, 1987), 3.

6. The proceedings of the conference constitute *Dreiser Studies* 21, no. 2 (Fall 1990).

Selected Bibliography

PRIMARY WORKS

Original Manuscripts

The majority of Dreiser's manuscripts reside in the Dreiser Collection of the University of Pennsylvania Library in Philadelphia. Dreiser personally deposited his papers there, and additional papers were added after his death by Helen Dreiser. Included are manuscripts of the majority of his books; galley and page proofs; first, subsequent, and foreign editions of the novels; correspondence; notes and worksheets; clipping files; portraits and busts by a variety of artists; and miscellany.

Other important collections are held at Lilly Library, Indiana University (Bloomington), which has the manuscript of *Dawn;* at the New York Public Library, which has the manuscript of *Sister Carrie;* at Enoch Pratt Free Library in Baltimore; at the Library of Cornell University, which has the collection of Dreiserana originally belonging to Robert H. Elias; and at the University of Virginia, which has the typescript of *Jennie Gerhardt.*

Novels

An American Tragedy. New York: Boni & Liveright, 1925.

The Bulwark. Garden City, N.Y.: Doubleday, 1946.

The Financier. New York: Harper, 1912. Rev. ed. New York: Boni & Liveright, 1927.

The "Genius." New York: John Lane Co., 1915.

Jennie Gerhardt. New York: Harper, 1911.

Sister Carrie. New York: Doubleday, Page, 1900.

Sister Carrie. Philadelphia: University of Pennsylvania Press, 1981. (The authoritative edition.)

The Stoic. Garden City, N.Y.: Doubleday, 1947.

The Titan. New York: John Lane Co., 1914.

Stories and Collections

The Best Short Stories of Theodore Dreiser. Edited by Howard Fast. Cleveland: World, 1947.

The Best Short Stories of Theodore Dreiser. Edited by James T. Farrell. Cleveland: World, 1956.

Chains. New York: Boni & Liveright, 1927.

Fine Furniture. New York: Random House, 1930.

Free, and Other Stories. New York: Boni & Liveright, 1918.

Drama

The Hand of the Potter. New York: Boni & Liveright, 1918.

Plays of the Natural and the Supernatural. New York: John Lane Co., 1916.

Poetry

The Aspirant. New York: Random House, 1929.

Epitaph: A Poem. New York: Heron Press, 1930.

Moods, Cadenced and Declaimed. New York: Boni & Liveright, 1928. Rev. ed. New York: Simon & Schuster, 1935.

My City. New York: Horace Liveright, 1929.

Autobiography

An Amateur Laborer. Edited by Richard W. Dowell. Philadelphia: University of Pennsylvania Press, 1983.

American Diaries, 1902-1926. Edited by Thomas P. Riggio. Philadelphia: University of Pennsylvania Press, 1982.

A Book about Myself. New York: Boni & Liveright, 1922 (editions beyond the seventh appear as *Newspaper Days*).

Dawn. New York: Liveright, 1931.

A Hoosier Holiday. New York: John Lane Company, 1916.

Newspaper Days. Edited by T. D. Nostwich. Philadelphia: University of Pennsylvania Press, 1991.

A Traveler at Forty. New York: Century, 1913.

Letters

Dreiser-Mencken Letters. Edited by Thomas P. Riggio. Philadelphia: University of Pennsylvania Press, 1986.

Letters of Theodore Dreiser. Edited by Robert H. Elias. 3 vols. Philadelphia: University of Pennsylvania Press, 1959.

Letters to Louise. Edited by Louise Campbell. Philadelphia: University of Pennsylvania Press, 1959.

Nonfiction

America Is Worth Saving. New York: Modern Age Books, 1941.

The Color of a Great City. New York: Boni & Liveright, 1923.

Dreiser Looks at Russia. New York: Boni & Liveright, 1928.

A Gallery of Women. New York: Boni & Liveright, 1929.

Hey, Rub-a-Dub-Dub! New York: Boni & Liveright, 1920.

Notes on Life. Edited by Marguerite Tjader and John J. McAleer. University: University of Alabama Press, 1974.

Selected Magazine Articles of Theodore Dreiser. Edited by Yoshinobu Hakutani. Rutherford, N.J.: Fairleigh Dickinson University Press, 1985 and 1987.

A Selection of Uncollected Prose. Edited by Donald Pizer. Detroit: Wayne State University Press, 1977.

"Theodore Dreiser." In *Living Philosophies.* Edited by Henry Goddard Leach, 55-77. New York: Simon & Schuster, 1931. Dreiser's own history of wondering and groping after some "meaning" in life, ending, he says, in this "summation of my lack of beliefs and faith."

Theodore Dreiser Journalism. Edited by T. D. Nostwich. Philadelphia: University of Pennsylvania Press, 1988.

Theodore Dreiser's "Heard in the Corridors" Articles and Related Writings. Edited by T. D. Nostwich. Ames: Iowa State University Press, 1988.

Tragic America. New York: Liveright, 1931.

Twelve Men. New York: Boni & Liveright, 1919.

SECONDARY WORKS

Bibliographies

Boswell, Jeanetta. *Theodore Dreiser and the Critics, 1911-1982.* Metuchen, N.J.: Scarecrow Press, 1986.

Pizer, Donald, Richard W. Dowell, and Frederic E. Rusch. *Theodore Dreiser: A Primary Bibliography and Reference Guide.* 2d ed. Boston: G. K. Hall & Co., 1991.

Biography, Books

Dreiser, Helen. *My Life with Dreiser.* Cleveland: World, 1951. A valuable if understandably subjective view of Dreiser by his widow.

Dreiser, Vera. *My Uncle Theodore.* New York: Nash, 1976. An account by the novelist's niece, a clinical psychologist.

Dudley, Dorothy. *Forgotten Frontiers: Dreiser and the Land of the Free.* New York: Harrison Smith & Robert Haas, 1932. The first sizable Dreiser biography, by a woman who clearly adored Dreiser and worked directly with him as she wrote.

Elias, Robert H. *Theodore Dreiser: Apostle of Nature.* New York: Knopf, 1949. Rev. ed. Ithaca, N.Y.: Cornell University Press, 1970. The first scholarly biography, written with Dreiser's cooperation. To date, the best single book on Dreiser.

Kennell, Ruth Epperson. *Theodore Dreiser and the Soviet Union 1927-1945.* New York: International, 1969. A first-hand chronicle by the woman who in 1927 served as Dreiser's guide/secretary during his visit to Russia.

Lingeman, Richard. *Theodore Dreiser: An American Journey 1908-1945.* New York: G. P. Putnam's Sons, 1990. The second and final volume of a highly respected biography based on recent scholarship.

_____. *Theodore Dreiser: At the Gates of the City 1871-1907.* New York: G. P. Putnam's Sons, 1986. The first volume of the Lingeman biography.

Lunden, Rolf. *Dreiser Looks at Scandinavia.* Stockholm: Almqvist & Wiksell, 1977. A detailed account of Dreiser's 1926 visit to Europe based upon his diaries.

Rascoe, Burton. *Theodore Dreiser.* New York: McBride, 1925. The first Dreiser biography, still valuable for its insights by a critic who knew the novelist.

Swanberg, W. A. *Dreiser.* New York: Scribner's, 1965. The most complete biography, and an indispensable reference for the reader who wishes to have the facts.

Tjader, Marguerite. *Theodore Dreiser: A New Dimension.* Norwalk, Conn.: Silvermine, 1965. Dreiser's life as seen and participated in by a volunteer editor; reads well in conjunction with Helen Dreiser's memoir.

Biography, Parts of Books

Anderson, Sherwood. "Dreiser's Party." In *Sherwood Anderson's Memoirs.* New York: Harcourt, Brace, 1924. Valuable for its detailed portrait of Dreiser at the time of his first meeting with Sherwood Anderson.

Boyd, Ernest. "Theodore Dreiser." In *Portraits: Real and Imaginary.* New York: George H. Doran, 1924. An interview written during Dreiser's Greenwich Village days.

Butcher, Fanny. *Many Lives – One Love.* New York: Harper & Row, 1972. Speaks of Dreiser's 1914 visit to Chicago and connections with the Little Theatre group.

Churchill, Allen. "Those Dreiserian Waves." *The Literary Decade.* Englewood Cliffs, N.J.: Prentice-Hall, 1971. Dreiser and his publisher Horace Liveright.

Deal, Borden. *The Tobacco Men.* New York: Holt, Rinehart & Winston, 1965. Contains foreword by Hy Kraft concerning his collaboration with Dreiser (1931-32) on a screenplay about the tobacco wars in turn-of-the-century Kentucky.

Frohock, W. M. "Theodore Dreiser." In *American Writers,* vol. 1., 497-520. New York: Scribner's, 1974. Brief and comprehensive biographical account.

Gerber, Philip L. "Dreiser's *Stoic:* A Study in Literary Frustration." In *Literary Monographs,* edited by Eric Rothstein and Joseph Wittreich, Jr., vol. 7, 85-144. Madison: University of Wisconsin Press, 1975. Concentrates on Dreiser's later years, from the 1930s until his death, while he tried to complete *The Stoic*.

———. "Theodore Dreiser." In *Dictionary of Literary Biography*, vol. 9, *American Novelists, 1910-1945*, 236-257. Detroit: Gale, 1981. Brief and comprehensive biographical account.

Gilmer, Walker. *Horace Liveright: Publisher of the Twenties*. New York: Lewis, 1970. Deals extensively with Dreiser and his chief publisher.

Hakutani, Yoshinobu. *Young Dreiser*. Rutherford, N.J.: Fairleigh Dickinson University Press, 1980. A brief and engaging account of Dreiser's life and career to the writing of *Sister Carrie* in 1900.

Harris, Frank. "Theodore Dreiser." In *Contemporary Portraits (Second Series)*. New York: Harris, 1919. A valuable early portrait based on interviews.

Jaeger, Clara. *Philadelphia Rebel*. Richmond, Va.: Grosvenor, 1988. An account of Dreiser's life during the 1930s by a lover/editor who worked for him as he struggled to complete *The Stoic*.

Putzel, Max. *The Man in the Mirror*. Cambridge: Harvard University Press, 1963. Contains references to Dreiser throughout, as well as a pair of discrete chapters, one on Dreiser, another on Dreiser and Harris Merton Lyon.

Rascoe, Burton. *We Were Interrupted*. Garden City, N.Y.: Doubleday, 1947. Accounts of Dreiser during the early 1920s by his journalist/critic friend.

Reynolds, Quentin. *The Fiction Factory*. New York: Random House, 1955. Includes data concerning Dreiser's employment by Street & Smith during the years following *Sister Carrie*.

Richards, Grant. *Author Hunting*. New York: Coward-McCann, 1934. Details the Richards-Dreiser connection both during Dreiser's 1911 trip to Europe and afterwards.

Sinclair, Upton. "An American Victory." *Money Talks*. New York: Albert & Charles Boni, 1927. A brief biographical essay on Dreiser, "the idol of our young writers today."

Criticism, Books

Brandon, Craig. *Murder in the Adirondacks*. Utica, N.Y.: North Country Books, 1986. The definitive study of sources for *An American Tragedy*.

Gerber, Philip L. *Plots and Characters in the Fiction of Theodore Dreiser*. Hamden, Conn.: Shoe String Press, 1977. A summary of plots and descriptive compendium of all characters in Dreiser's fiction.

Griffin, Joseph. *The Small Canvas*. Rutherford, N.J.: Fairleigh Dickinson University Press, 1985. Unique in its concentration on Dreiser's short fiction.

Hussman, Lawrence E., Jr. *Dreiser and His Fiction: A Twentieth-Century Quest.* Philadelphia: University of Pennsylvania Press, 1983. A fine study of Dreiser's fiction, stressing its essential morality and Dreiser's themes of responsibility and culpability.

Lehan, Richard. *Theodore Dreiser.* Carbondale: University of Southern Illinois Press, 1969. A comprehensive study of Dreiser's novels within a biographical frame.

Lunden, Rolf. *The Inevitable Equation.* Stockholm: Rotobeckman, 1973. An extensive treatment of Dreiser's philosophy based on the manuscripts of his "Notes on Life."

Lundquist, James. *Theodore Dreiser.* New York: Unger, 1974. A concise study emphasizing Dreiser's use of deterministic philosophy.

McAleer, John J. *Theodore Dreiser.* New York: Holt, Rinehart & Winston, 1968. A useful introduction, combining Dreiser's biography with interpretations of his novels.

Matthiessen, F. O. *Theodore Dreiser.* New York: William Sloane, 1951. An excellent critical biography for the general reader.

Moers, Ellen. *Two Dreisers.* New York: Viking, 1969. A superb and penetrating study of *Sister Carrie* and *An American Tragedy.*

Mookerjee, R. N. *Theodore Dreiser: His Thought and Social Criticism.* Delhi: National Publishing House, 1974. Valuable for its insights into Dreiser's social thought from an Indian critic's viewpoint.

Mukherjee, Arun. *The Gospel of Wealth in the American Novel.* Totowa, N.J.: Barnes & Noble, 1987. The dilemma of the writer in a capitalistic society, largely devoted to Dreiser.

Pizer, Donald. *The Novels of Theodore Dreiser.* Minneapolis: University of Minnesota Press, 1976. An admirable study of Dreiser's novels and the circumstances surrounding their composition.

Shapiro, Charles. *Theodore Dreiser: Our Bitter Patriot.* Carbondale: Southern Illinois University Press, 1962. A study of Dreiser's fiction according to the theme of "a society which tantalizes but never produces."

Warren, Robert Penn. *Homage to Theodore Dreiser.* New York: Random House, 1971. An important American novelist pays tribute to Dreiser's ability to craft an outstanding body of fiction from his life and times.

West, James L. W. III. *A Sister Carrie Portfolio.* Charlottesville: University Press of Virginia, 1985. A fascinating compilation of facts, photographs, and facsimiles concerning the composition and publication of *Sister Carrie.*

Criticism, Collections

Gerber, Philip L., ed. *Dreiser Studies* 11, no.2 (Fall 1980). A special issue devoted to the proceedings of the Brockport Conference (October 1990), titled "Working Girls: Dreiser's *Sister Carrie* at Ninety."

Kazin, Alfred, and Charles Shapiro, eds. *The Stature of Theodore Dreiser* (Bloomington: Indiana University Press, 1955).

Pizer, Donald, ed. *Critical Essays on Theodore Dreiser*. Boston: G. K. Hall, 1981. Thirty-seven essays representing a wide variety of Dreiser criticism since c. 1914. Supersedes *The Stature of Theodore Dreiser* by Kazin and Shapiro (1955).

_____. *New Essays on Sister Carrie*. New York: Cambridge University Press, 1991.

Raja, L. Jeganatha, ed. *The Journal of Life, Art and Literature* 3, no. 1 (January 1984). A special number on Dreiser that includes a variety of essays by American and Indian scholars.

_____. *Theodore Dreiser: The Man and His Message*. Annamalainagar: Kathy, 1984. An expansion of the preceding entry.

Salzman, Jack, ed. *Modern Fiction Studies*, 23, no. 3 (Autumn 1977). A special number devoted to essays by a wide variety of Dreiser scholars and biographers.

_____. *Theodore Dreiser: The Critical Reception*. New York: Lewis, 1972. A valuable compilation of contemporary newspaper and magazine reviews of Dreiser's books.

West, James L. W. III, ed. *Papers on Language and Literature* 27, no. 2 (Spring 1991). A special number containing 10 essays, ranging from a study of Dreiser's handwriting to a consideration of the creative process that led to *The Financier*.

Criticism, Parts of Books

Blankenship, Russell. "Theodore Dreiser." In *American Literature as an Expression of the National Mind*. New York: Holt, 1935. A friendly reappraisal of Dreiser in mid-career.

Brooks, Van Wyck. "Theodore Dreiser." In *The Confident Years: 1885-1915*. New York: Dutton, 1951. Dreiser seen as the product of his environment, a man whose ability to convey actuality in his novels triumphed over literary weaknesses.

Conder, John J. *Naturalism in American Fiction: The Classic Phase*. Lexington: University of Kentucky Press, 1984. Deals with the Cowperwood trilogy as a prime example of deterministic thinking.

Drummond, Edward J., S.J. "Theodore Dreiser: Shifting Naturalism." In *Fifty Years of the American Novel*, edited by Harold C. Gardiner. New York: Scribner's, 1951. A Catholic appraisal of the complexities and paradoxes in Dreiser's evolving thought.

Edgar, Pelham. "American Realism, Sex, and Theodore Dreiser." *The Art of the Novel*. New York: Macmillan, 1933. A British appreciation, comparing Dreiser with Zola.

Farrell, James T. "Dreiser's *Sister Carrie*." In *The League of Frightened Philistines*. New York: Vanguard, 1945. Explains why *Sister Carrie* is an American classic.

_____. "Theodore Dreiser: In Memoriam." In *Literature and Morality*. New York: Vanguard, 1947. An appreciation of Dreiser as "the great novelist of the period of capitalistic growth and expansion."

Fisher, Philip. "The Life History of Objects: The Naturalist Novel and the City." In *Hard Facts*. New York: Oxford University Press, 1985. A highly perceptive analysis of Dreiser's "intuitive genius" at work capturing the essence of urbanized American society in *Sister Carrie* and *An American Tragedy*.

Fishkin, Shelley Fisher. "Theodore Dreiser." In *From Fact to Fiction*. New York: Oxford University Press, 1985. Explores the connections between Dreiser's fiction and his apprenticeship in journalism.

Geismar, Maxwell. "Theodore Dreiser: The Double Soul." In *Rebels and Ancestors: The American Novel, 1890-1915*. Boston: Houghton Mifflin, 1953. A detailed analysis, valuable for its insights into Dreiser's methods and intentions.

Gelfant, Blanche. "Theodore Dreiser: The Portrait Novel." In *The American City Novel*. Norman: University of Oklahoma Press, 1954. Dreiser as a key figure in fiction of the American city.

Grebstein, Sheldon N. "Theodore Dreiser." In *The Politics of Twentieth-Century Novelists*, edited by George A. Panichas. New York: Hawthorn, 1971. Equating politics with power and force, Grebstein demonstrates the manner in which these concerns permeate Dreiser's fiction.

Hapke, Laura. *Tales of the Working Girl*. New York: Twayne Publishers, 1992.

Kazin, Alfred. *On Native Grounds*. New York: Reynal & Hitchcock, 1942. A landmark study of Dreiser's emergence and his unique contribution.

Lee, Brian. "Realism and Naturalism: Howells, Crane, Norris, Dreiser." In *American Fiction 1965-1940*. New York: Longman, 1987. A British view of the "laureate" of Chicago and the American Midwest.

Lydenberg, John. "Theodore Dreiser: Ishmael in the Jungle." In *American Radicals*, edited by Harvey Goldberg. New York: Monthly Review Press, 1957. Concentrates on Dreiser's special position as an "outsider" in American society and his unsuccessful battle to remain politically neutral.

Martin, Jay. *Harvests of Change: American Literature 1865-1914*. Englewood Cliffs, N.J.: Prentice-Hall, 1967. Praises Dreiser for his unusual receptivity to both the surface and the significant themes of the society in which he lived.

Mencken, H. L. "The American Novel." In *Prejudices: Fourth Series.* New York: Knopf, 1924. Strong presentation of Dreiser's influence in freeing American writing and in making the novel "true."

————. "Theodore Dreiser." In *A Book of Prefaces.* New York: Knopf, 1917. An early and intense apologia by Dreiser's first great admirer.

Michaels, Walter Benn. "Sister Carrie's Popular Economy" and "Dreiser's Financier: The Man of Business as a Man of Letters." In *The Gold Standard and the Logic of Naturalism: American Literature at the Turn of the Century* (Berkeley: University of California Press, 1987). Provocative readings of Dreiser's novels as they relate to the history of American capitalism.

Parrington, Vernon. "Theodore Dreiser: Chief of American Naturalists." In *Main Currents in American Thought,* vol. 3. New York: Harcourt, Brace, 1930. A sympathetic analysis of Dreiser's literary philosophy and method, the most "frank and detached projection of reality" since Whitman.

Poirier, Richard. *A World Elsewhere.* London: Chatto & Windus, 1967. An unusual addition to Dreiser studies, concluding that Dreiser, stylistically, is in "the strongest tradition of American literature."

Spiller, Robert E. "Theodore Dreiser." In *Literary History of the United States.* New York: Macmillan, 1948. A most useful and comprehensive summary of Dreiser's life, works, ideas, and methods.

Van Doren, Carl. "Theodore Dreiser." In *The American Novel.* New York: Macmillan, 1940. Discusses the reasons for Dreiser's "permanent place in American fiction" despite early public and critical disapproval.

Wagenknecht, Edward. "Theodore Dreiser, the Mystic Naturalist." In *The Cavalcade of the American Novel.* New York: Holt, 1952. Demonstrates that Dreiser worked within a wider spectrum of ideas than the purely naturalistic.

Walcutt, Charles Child. "Theodore Dreiser: The Wonder and Terror of Life." In *American Literary Naturalism, A Divided Stream.* Minneapolis: University of Minnesota Press, 1956. Traces the changes and contradictions in Dreiser's ideas, leading to "the most moving and powerful novels of the naturalistic tradition."

Waldman, Milton. "Theodore Dreiser." In *Contemporary American Authors,* edited by J. C. Squire. New York: Holt, 1928. Surveys Dreiser's novels with the usual 1920s emphasis on his stylistic shortcomings, yet concludes that Dreiser has achieved a vivid "picture of the dynamic but inarticulate community about him."

West, James L. W. III. "Theodore Dreiser." In *Sixteen Modern American Authors, Volume 2,* edited by Jackson R. Bryer. Durham: Duke University Press, 1990. The most recent update of this indispensable review of scholarship concerning Dreiser bibliography, biography, and criticism.

Ziff, Larzer. "A Decade's Delay." In *The American 1890s*. New York: Viking, 1966. Explains Dreiser's survival as the major novelist of a generation that included Frank Norris and Stephen Crane.

Criticism, Periodicals

Anderson, Sherwood. "An Apology for Crudity." *Dial*, 8 November 1917, 437-38. Notable as an early defense of Dreiser and his rejection of slick writing and mechanical plotting.

Bourne, Randolph. "Theodore Dreiser," *New Republic*, 17 April 1915, Supplement 7-8. An early defense of Dreiser as a writer one can read "without shame and embarrassment" because of his utterly truthful portrayal of life.

Dowell, Richard W. "Dreiser's Courtship Letters: Portents of a Doomed Marriage." *Dreiser Newsletter*, Spring 1984, 14-20. An examination of 69 letters, long unavailable, from Dreiser to Sara White, whom he later married.

Flint, R. W. "Dreiser: The Press of Life." *Nation*. 27 April 1957, 371-73. An estimate of Dreiser as "*the* great American novelist of his time and place."

Gerber, Philip L. "The Alabaster Protegéee: Dreiser and Berenice Fleming" *American Literature*, May 1971, 217-30. Traces the life and character of Emilie Grigsby, the prototype of Berenice Fleming in *The Titan* and *The Stoic*.

_____. "Dreiser's Financier: A Genesis." *Journal of Modern Literature*, March 1971, 354-74. Traces the life and career of Charles T. Yerkes, the prototype of Frank Cowperwood, indicating sources Dreiser used in writing *The Financier* and other novels.

_____. "The Financier Himself: Dreiser and C. T. Yerkes," *PMLA*, January 1973, 112-21. Cites those traits of Charles T. Yerkes which Dreiser incorporated into the character of Frank Cowperwood, explaining why it was that Yerkes was selected as the archetypical financier.

_____. "Frank Cowperwood: Boy Financier." *Studies in American Fiction*, August 1974, 165-74. Examines the first chapters of *The Financier* to demonstrate the use Dreiser made of the life of Charles T. Yerkes in his fictional portrayal.

_____. "Cowperwood Treads the Boards." *Dreiser Newsletter*, Fall 1983, 8-17. Examines the efforts of a Dreiser admirer to adapt the Cowperwood novels to the stage during the 1920s.

Graham, Don B. "Aesthetic Experience in Realism." *American Literary Realism*, Winter 1975, 289-90. Argues that prior to the "demeublization" of the novel, the highly detailed novel was a typical and admired genre.

_____. "Dreiser and Thoreau: An Early Influence." *Dreiser Newsletter*, Spring 1976, 1-4. Demonstrates that Dreiser had in mind Thoreau's chapter "Brute Neighbors" when he composed his early story "The Shining Slave Makers."

Grebstein, Sheldon N. "Dreiser's Victorian Vamp." *Midcontinent American Studies Journal*, 1963, 3-12. Carrie Meeber is seen as a stereotypical Victorian mixture of strengths and weaknesses who yields sexually but has no passion of her own.

Hussman, Lawrence E. "Thomas Edison and *Sister Carrie:* A Source for Character and Theme." *American Literary Naturalism*, Spring 1975, 155-58. Argues that the character of Robert Ames in *Sister Carrie* is probably based on the inventor Thomas Edison, whom Dreiser had interviewed.

_____. "A Measure of Sister Carrie's Growth." *Dreiser Newsletter*, Spring 1980, 13-23. Concludes that Dreiser did little to indicate growth and change in Carrie Meeber, despite his obvious intention to use the character of Robert Ames in order to achieve such an end.

Hutchisson, James. "The Composition and Publication of 'Another American Tragedy': Dreiser's 'Typhoon,' " *Papers of the Bibliographic Society of America*, 1987, 25-35. Establishes the authoritative text of "Typhoon" as well as the history of its composition.

Kwiat, Joseph J. "Dreiser's *The 'Genius'* and Everett Shinn, 'The Ashcan Painter.' " *PMLA*, March 1952, 15-31. Establishes Dreiser's knowledge of the painter Shinn and argues that the character of Eugene Witla is based largely upon him.

_____. "The Newspaper Experience: Crane, Norris, and Dreiser." *Nineteenth-Century Fiction*, September 1953, 99-117. Examines Dreiser's journalistic apprenticeship for its influences upon his writing of fiction.

Mencken, H. L. "The Creed of a Novelist." *Smart Set*, October 1916, 138-43. An early defense of Dreiser by his foremost supporter.

Moers, Ellen. "The Finesse of Dreiser." *American Scholar*, Winter 1963, 109-14. A pioneering investigation into the notion that Dreiser's style is defensible and even skillful.

Mookerjee, R. N. "Dreiser's Use of Hindu Thought in *The Stoic*." *American Literature*, May 1971, 273-78. Examines Dreiser's interest in Hindu ideas and his use of the *Bhagavad Gita* in *The Stoic*.

Nostwich, Theodore D. "The Source of Dreiser's 'Nigger Jeff.' " *Resources for American Literary Study*, Autumn 1978, 174-87. Argues that Dreiser based his story not on a lynching he attended but on articles appearing in the Saint Louis *Republic* in 1894.

Orlov, Paul A. "The Subversion of the Self: Anti-Naturalistic Crux in *An American Tragedy*." *Modern Fiction Studies*, Fall 1977, 457-72. A revisionist view that argues that Dreiser views man as less of a helpless victim of heredity and environment than is generally supposed.

_____. "Plot as Parody: Dreiser's Attack on the Alger Theme in *An American Tragedy*." *American Literary Realism*, Autumn 1982, 239-43. Sees *An American Tragedy* as an ironic inversion of the Horatio Alger rags-to-riches formula and thus an outright attack on the success motive in American life.

Phillips, William L. "The Imagery of Dreiser's Novels." *PMLA*, December 1963, 572-85. A relatively early effort to indicate Dreiser's artistry in the use of images of water, animals, and fairyland to buttress the central ideas contained in his novels.

Riggio, Thomas P. "American Gothic: Poe and *An American Tragedy*." *American Literature*, 1978, 515-32. Quotes from Poe to indicate that Dreiser drew from that source for various images in his novel.

_____. "Dreiser on Society and Literature: The San Francisco Exposition Interview." *American Literary Realism*, 1978, 284-94. Prints for the first time an interview that took place in 1939, with Dreiser reflecting on American society.

_____. "The Dreisers in Sullivan: A Biographical Revision." *Dreiser Newsletter*, Fall 1979, 1-12. An examination of Dreiser's account of his youth in Sullivan, Indiana, focusing on his probably exaggerated portrait of his father as a habitual failure.

Ross, Woodburn O. "Concerning Dreiser's Mind." *American Literature*, November 1946, 233-43. Attacks the position held by Mencken and others that Dreiser is not a thoroughgoing mechanist, that "one-half of the man's brain, so to speak, wars with the other half."

Stewart, Randall. "Dreiser and the Naturalistic Heresy." *Virginia Quarterly Review*, Winter 1958, 100-116. A latter-day attack on the naturalistic view as being an untenable philosophy of life.

Weir, Sybil B. "The Image of Women in Dreiser's Fiction, 1900-1925." *Pacific Coast Philology*, April 1972, 65-71. Presents Dreiser as "the first, and perhaps the only, major American novelist" to treat the sexual lives of women in the same manner as those of men.

Williams, Philip. "The Chapter Titles of *Sister Carrie*." *American Literature*, November 1964, 359-65. Reveals that the chapter titles were a late addition to Dreiser's manuscript, probably as a means of making the book more acceptable to publishers; then discusses the titles in terms of imagery.

Witemeyer, Hugh. "Gaslight and Magic Lamp in *Sister Carrie*." *PMLA*. May 1972, 236-40. Examines Dreiser's use of the theater to underscore the dichotomy between illusion and reality.

Index

The Author

Philip Gerber, professor of English at the State University of New York, is the author of *Robert Frost* and *Willa Cather*, both in Twayne's United States Authors Series. He has published *Plots and Characters in the Fiction of Theodore Dreiser* as well as a number of composition texts. His most recent book is *Bachelor Bess: The Homesteading Letters of Elizabeth Corey, 1909-1919*. Professor Gerber has served as president of the New York state branches of the American Studies Association and the College English Association, and he is a member of the Editorial Board for the University of Pennsylvania edition of Theodore Dreiser. In 1989 Gerber was president of the Robert Frost Society and in 1990 was the recipient of the MidAmerica Award for distinguished contributions to the study of midwestern literature.

The Editor

Joseph M. Flora earned his B.A. (1956), M.A. (1957), and Ph.D. (1962) in English at the University of Michigan. In 1962 he joined the faculty of the University of North Carolina, where he is now professor of English. His study *Hemingway's Nick Adams* (1984) won the Mayflower Award. He is also author of *Vardis Fisher* (1962), *William Ernest Henley* (1970), *Frederick Manfred* (1974), and *Ernest Hemingway: A Study of the Short Fiction* (1989). He is editor of *The English Short Story* (1985) and coeditor of *Southern Writers: A Biographical Dictionary* (1970), *Fifty Southern Writers before 1900* (1987), and *Fifty Southern Writers after 1900* (1987). He serves on the editorial boards of *Studies in Short Fiction* and *Southern Literary Journal*.